FINDING A JOB IN YOUR FIELD

A Handbook for Ph.D.'s and M.A.'s

Rebecca Anthony and Gerald Roe

D1445803

Peterson's Guides
Princeton, New Jersey

Library of Congress Cataloging in Publication Data

Anthony, Rebecca, 1950–
        Finding a job in your field.

        Bibliography: p.
        Includes index.

        1. Graduate students—Employment. 2. Job hunting.
I. Roe, Gerald. II. Title.
HD6277.A57   1984   650.1'4   84-9594
ISBN 0-87866-278-2

Printed in the United States of America

10 9 8 7 6 5 4 3 2 1

For information about other Peterson's publications, please see the listing at the back of this volume.

To our children—
Natalya, Natassia, and Veronica
Stephen and David

Contents

Introduction

Finding a Job in Your Field is for people with advanced degrees who wish to obtain academic or other professional positions commensurate with their education, abilities, and interests. As a result of a combination of demographic and economic factors—declining undergraduate enrollments, financial constraints on both public and private institutions, and the enormous increase in the number of graduate degrees awarded since the 1970s—advanced degree holders in many fields face a crowded and highly competitive market. As a result, in spite of the plentiful (though often conflicting) advice you receive from well-meaning friends, colleagues, and family members, you may find the process of finding a job in your field confusing and frustrating, whether you are a novice or a veteran.

If you are seeking your first job, you are probably in the process of completing an advanced degree or have recently finished your program of study. Unless you entered a library study carrel at the beginning of your program, emerging only for classes and seminars, you have probably spent some time in the department lounge or other favorite hangout where the conversation of your peers inevitably has turned to the frustrations, pitfalls, and joys of job seeking. By listening to others talk about their experiences you have probably absorbed a good deal of information, but do not assume that you know through osmosis how to conduct a job search. Even those who have been through the process usually believe they need more information before beginning another search.

Finding a job in your field is a goal worthy of energetic and determined pursuit. Career plans should not be made lightly or without appropriate deliberation. The decisions you make and the career direction you follow will have substantial immediate and long-range implications. Although we believe that an individual can be challenged and fulfilled by more than one career path, we recognize that the essence of any work experience becomes a fundamentally important part of one's life. For most of us, the degree of satisfaction we find in our careers contributes to the success of our personal and social relationships.

Any job search will be influenced, of course, by the availability of positions and the number of competitors for each opening. Some fields have an almost desperate demand for qualified people; in others, the supply of qualified people far exceeds the demand for their services. Whatever your particular field of study, whatever the amount of competition you face, you can learn to use job-seeking techniques and employment tactics that will increase your chances for success. While you can't change the numbers, you can change the odds.

Finding a Job in Your Field demystifies the processes of designing academic vitas and professional résumés, of writing effective cover letters, preparing for and successfully interviewing with search committees and hiring officials, and expanding the options related to your preparation, background, and skills. Each chapter explains and illustrates steps and procedures by which people are selected for positions. Individuals with advanced degrees from the master's through the doctorate can use this book to formulate and carry out an orderly and purposeful job search whether they are seeking their first job or a new and better professional position.

Our work at The University of Iowa brings us into daily contact with new Ph.D.'s and M.A.'s seeking their first academic or professional positions and with alumni attempting to advance their careers by finding new jobs in new locations. Through group seminars and individual conferences, we assist students and alumni to identify employment possibilities, to understand the selection process, to control information presented to potential employers, and to feel satisfied that they have done all they can to conduct an effective and productive job search. Our experience tells us that knowledgeable and organized job seekers are far more likely to achieve their goals than those who approach the job search, as many do, haphazardly and without a full understanding of the procedures and techniques required for success.

Because there was no publication addressing the unique needs of these people, we wrote this book to provide assistance to those of you seeking academic and professional jobs—the preparations for which already have cost you thousands of dollars and years of time. We hope this book will answer your questions, allay your anxieties, and allow you to approach your job search with a clear understanding of what potential employers will expect of you at each stage of the selection process and with confidence in your ability to find a job that offers both personal and professional rewards.

Chapter One

Organizing Your Job Search

Most Ph.D.'s and M.A.'s feel very uncomfortable with the idea of "selling themselves" to potential employers. Unfortunately, in today's market an advanced degree can no longer be considered a ticket to a career. It is essential for new graduates as well as experienced professionals to develop a thorough, well-defined plan to promote their skills, qualifications, experiences, and personalities. You undoubtedly feel confident that the knowledge and competencies acquired in graduate school have prepared you for a professional position. However, sophisticated as you may be about the intricacies of your chosen field, you may feel inadequately prepared and uneasy about the prospect of finding suitable employment opportunities and getting hired in a competitive market.

It's not that you're afraid of competition. You have competed for grades and recognition throughout your graduate school experience, but the competition you now face for available positions in your field will undoubtedly be even more intense and, for most individuals, will have far greater consequences. Like your graduate program, the process by which people are selected for academic and professional positions can be seen as a linear progression. Unlike your graduate studies, however, which were designed in such a way that successful completion of each stage of the outlined program would lead you that much closer to your goal, the course of your job search must usually be determined and executed on your own, relying on your own judgment and your own particular skills, and adapted to your unique preferences and requirements. This chapter will outline what you need to know and what you need to do to organize an efficient and effective job search.

One of the first and most obvious questions for beginning job seekers and experienced professionals alike is, "When do I start my job search?" It is not possible for most individuals to pinpoint a specific moment to launch a campaign, nor does everyone begin in exactly the same way. Some people begin a job search only when they hear of a position for which they would like to be considered; others begin by preparing paperwork which will be required in the course of the employment process. Although not everyone follows precisely the same sequence of steps, students usually begin to think seriously about job seeking once they

1

have completed a substantial portion of the work for an advanced degree. Candidates for the doctorate often begin to look for positions during the year in which course work and comprehensive examinations will be completed, with the intention of finishing the dissertation while employed. Both students and working professionals need to allow sufficient time for a job search; preparations should be made several months before the expected starting date of a new position.

Whether you are currently completing your degree, finishing your dissertation, holding down a full-time nonrelated job, or already involved in an academic or other professional position, a job search may prove enormously difficult without exceptional organizational skills. While it is not possible to predict the exact amount of time and energy that must be devoted to finding a job, most graduate students feel that job seeking is at least the equivalent of adding another course to one's schedule. Add family responsibilities and the question of finding the necessary time to do a thorough job search becomes a serious consideration. In addition to the time spent in preparing applications, the problem of scheduling interviews compounds the difficulties. Establishing priorities for routine activities and allowing for the additional responsibilities of all the things that must be attended to in the job search are critical. Your ability to manage your time and direct your energies may be directly correlated to the degree of success you experience.

Beginning a job search without sufficient preparation may produce unpleasant side effects that include loss of self-esteem or loss of faith in the system, which can cripple your chances for success in this and future job searches. It may be necessary to resist the promptings and urgings of those close to you if you do not feel ready to undertake a job search. Those who attempt to find a job before they are ready to commit themselves and their resources to the business at hand risk the fruitless expenditure of time, energy, and money, and the accumulation of frustrations and doubts for themselves, family members, and mentors.

In addition to budgeting time, you will want to give serious consideration to the amount of money you will need to meet various expenses related to securing employment. The cost of a job search will be influenced by the availability of positions in your field and the scope of your search. The cash outlay required can be minimal or it can run to several thousand dollars. Typical expenses will include:

- Vita/Résumé Production. Costs depend upon quantity required and whether they are self-produced or commercially prepared.

- Supplies and Materials. Typewriter purchase or rental could be the largest single item in this category, but it is surprising how much money is needed for paper, stationery, envelopes, copying costs, and other miscellaneous items.

- Portfolio. Production and packaging of supporting materials such as slides of artwork, audio or video tapes, scores, programs, or writing samples can be a considerable expense.

- Postage. In addition to mailing cover letters and vitas, it is necessary to include return postage for portfolio materials.

- Placement and Dossier Service. Registration fees, membership dues, and subscriptions for vacancy listings will require a cash outlay. Placement fees for commercial placement agencies are usually based on a percentage of annual salary and can amount to several thousand dollars.

- Transcripts. Official copies of undergraduate and graduate records are often requested by search committees. Though individual costs may be negligible, the collective cost per application can be staggering if you have attended several colleges or universities.

- Telephone. Long-distance calls are unavoidable in most job searches. Almost all employment-related calls must be made at higher daytime rates and, though even more expensive, operator-assisted person-to-person calls may be the most economical in the long run.

- Interviews. Wardrobe expenses and conference registration fees can represent significant amounts of money. Travel, lodging, and food can necessitate a considerable cash outlay even if you are ultimately reimbursed for these expenses.

And don't forget moving expenses! Once you accept a position, the cost of transporting yourself, family members, and household goods and settling into a new community can be considerable. Some institutions are able to reimburse new employees for all or part of the expense of relocating, but that practice is far from universal. Be sure to plan ahead for the probability of a large cash outlay.

ORGANIZING AND COLLECTING ESSENTIAL MATERIALS

Aside from knowing that a job search will require time, energy, and money, you should anticipate some immediate steps that must be taken before you respond to your first vacancy notice or place your first phone call. To support your application for a position, you will need to collect and organize materials that document your education and experience. Among these items are letters of recommendation, transcripts, and pertinent samples of your work.

LETTERS OF RECOMMENDATION

Whether you are currently completing your degree or are already employed in your field, appropriate recommendations must be collected to be made available for review by potential employers. Search committees or other potential employers expect to receive letters of recommendation from people for whom you have worked and with whom you have studied. Important references may include:

- academic/dissertation adviser
- examining committee
- departmental faculty
- internship/practicum supervisor
- current and previous employers

Before you request letters of recommendation from these people, you should understand that the Family Educational Rights and Privacy Act of 1974, commonly known as the Buckley Amendment, provides that students at postsecondary institutions have the right to inspect and review their education records, including placement files maintained by college placement offices. The legislation further states that students must have the option to waive or retain the right of access to education records collected after January 1, 1975. As you begin the process of gathering recommendations, the decision must be made to waive or retain the right of access to the references requested.

Confidential recommendations have long been the tradition and the norm in academic employment. As a result of the Buckley Amendment, there has been a great deal of discussion about the validity of nonconfidential recommendations. Although the issue of confidentiality may be a possible factor in academic and professional employment, its effects cannot be isolated. Several years after implementation of the legislation, the controversy continues but little empirical data is available to support opinions or strong feelings on either side of the issue.

Do not misinterpret the meaning of the term "confidential." Simply put, if you waive your right of access to a reference, your placement office will not make it available for your inspection and review. The writer of the reference may share its content with you or even give you a copy of the statement, but he or she is not obligated to do so. Although some writers routinely share their statements with the individual requesting a reference, you should not expect that this will happen or be disappointed if it does not.

You may be motivated to retain the right of access to your references by several impressions or beliefs. Simple curiosity about the content of the reference may be a factor. The right of access may also be retained as a matter of principle. Some students feel that it is to their advantage to be aware of the content of the references so that they can anticipate interview questions from prospective employers or capitalize on the strengths emphasized in the recommendations. Others retain the right of access in order to refute or to request removal of a reference which they feel may not represent them to their best advantage. On the other hand, some job seekers waive the right of access due to the real or perceived impression that employers will consider confidential references more credible. Faculty members may influence or even intimidate students to waive the right of access either from personal preference or with the assumption that confidential references will increase the student's chance of finding employment.

Before making your decision, you may want to discuss the issue of confidentiality with the reference writers, your placement adviser, or your mentor. If you have any reservations about a reference, it will be better for you to retain the right of access so that you can be aware of its content. It is far better to retain your right than to spend needless hours of worry or frustration over the uncertainty of what the writer may have said about you or your qualifications. It must be understood by students, faculty, and employers that the content of the reference should be of far greater significance than the individual's decision to waive or retain the right of access.

DOSSIERS

Important as references can be, they do not stand alone but are accompanied by academic records and relevant professional data. This collection is referred to as a placement file, credential file, or dossier. Various offices or agencies may be able to assist you in establishing a dossier and can also provide related employment services.

Academic Departments. Some departments take a very active role in helping students find suitable employment by nominating students and recent graduates for specific jobs and writing individual letters supporting their students' applications for available positions. Some departments collect faculty references and send them to search committees or other potential employers at the request of students. Departments inform their students about such assistance through campus meetings or memos. Check with your adviser about departmental placement assistance.

College or University Placement Offices. Almost every college and university has established an office to assist students and alumni with career planning and placement. Typical services include job vacancy bulletins, credential or dossier service, vita and interview seminars, and career counseling and advice. Check with the placement office on your campus to determine the services available to you.

Professional Associations. Some associations provide placement services for their members. For individuals who have not yet completed their degrees, student memberships may be available at reduced cost. Such professional associations may offer vacancy listings and dossier services, and often coordinate vita dissemination and interview scheduling at regional and national conferences.

Commercial or Private Agencies. Services provided by private agencies range from putting out periodic vacancy bulletins to offering comprehensive placement programs that include résumé and vita preparation, referrals, and dossier submission. Before registering with the agency, inquire about available services and required fees.

It is not unusual for academics and professionals to use more than one of the offices or agencies mentioned above. When considering the various services offered, inquire about the costs and the terms of the available services.

Departments and college placement offices may offer services without charge or at moderate cost. Placement office fees vary with the institution and the types of services provided; if fees are required, some charge separately for dossier service and job listings and others charge a flat fee for all services. Each professional association offering placement assistance has established guidelines regarding services and fees. Some offer placement assistance only during scheduled conferences; others may operate on a year-round basis for dossier service and periodic job bulletins. Membership dues may be required in order to utilize placement services, and there may be additional fees for job bulletins and dossier submissions. Commercial placement agencies may charge for registration, placement, and maintenance. Registration fees are common; all registrants pay the same initial fee. Upon employment, placement fees may range from a flat rate to a commission based on a percentage of your first year's salary. If the file is to be maintained for future use, an annual fee may be required.

Because academic and professional positions are advertised and available throughout the year, it is important that your dossier be available at any time. Determine if placement service is available on a year-round basis or only at conferences. Find out the frequency of job bulletins. Ask if vacancy listings are offered on a weekly, monthly, quarterly, or annual basis. Consider also the duration and permanence of your dossier or placement file. Academic departments and some university offices tend to concentrate their efforts on placement of current students and recent graduates. Some offices and agencies destroy your records after a specified number of years; others retain your dossier indefinitely and provide for updating as your career progresses.

PERSONAL FILE

In addition to the dossier compiled by an office or agency, every job seeker should develop a personal file that includes transcripts, certificates, and copies of any forms submitted to a placement service. If you have been given copies of your letters of recommendation, or if you have obtained additional references from colleagues, character references, or student evaluations, these documents should be maintained in your personal file. Although it is not a common occurrence, items sent to or from your placement service can be misplaced, misfiled, or even lost in the mails. Having these materials readily available for your personal use allows you to work independently if you choose and can serve as a backup in emergencies.

PORTFOLIO

To complement the dossier and personal file, each job seeker needs to collect supplemental materials to be used in the applic___ ___n process. This collection is commonly referred to as a portfolio, a term ___ ___in the visual arts but applicable to any field. The exact nature of ___ ___ls depends upon your area of specialization and your job objectiv___ ___ any discipline should have writing samples ready for submission. J___ ___o have published articles should have reprints available. Dissertation___ ___mple chapters, and other major works relevant to the position for ___ ___e applying should be available for review by the search committee. ___ ___y, slides and audio and video tapes may be used by job seekers in a va___ ___s such as counseling, theater, journalism, music, physical education, ___ ___t, and graphics.

Portfolios should not be submi___ ___tically. If supporting materials are desired the vacancy notice will ___ ___est them or selected individuals will be invited to submit them at a la___ ___hen submitting portfolios, always enclose return postage and a self-addre___ ___velope to ensure their return. Because search committees may retain these materials for a considerable time, multiple copies are required. Careful inspection of any materials returned should be undertaken before they are circulated again. If any flaws are apparent, the item must be replaced. The impressions created by portfolios are too important to permit anything but the highest quality of reproduction and overall appearance.

IDENTIFYING JOB POSSIBILITIES

Once you have determined that you are ready to begin a job search and have begun to assemble the dossier and portfolio that will support your applications, you need to think about actual job possibilities. Your awareness and understanding of the various types of institutions and organizations that hire individuals with advanced degrees can allow you to assess the likelihood of your employment, to determine your priorities and preferences, and to devise appropriate employment strategies.

ACADEMIC OPPORTUNITIES

If you are seeking an academic position, employment possibilities can be explored at a wide range of institutions from small independent or church-affiliated colleges to the prestigious and highly selective private universities, from state-supported schools in rural areas to the huge metropolitan campuses. Your own educational experiences will undoubtedly influence your perceptions and attitudes about various kinds of postsecondary institutions. But restricting your job search only to the types of schools you have attended can unnecessarily limit your job search. Considering positions only in small, private liberal arts colleges or in schools affiliated with a particular philosophy or religion or assuming that you could only be stimulated and productive in a large public university serves to decrease the number of opportunities open to you. Obviously, you will want to work in an environment that you think will be compatible with your views and will allow you to exercise individual freedom, but you should not assume that only one type of institution offers that kind of flexibility. Considering all viable opportunities will allow you to apply for positions at academic institutions offering various levels of degrees.

Institutions Granting Graduate Degrees. Faculty members may teach graduate as well as undergraduate classes, conduct advanced seminars, and participate in supervision of theses and dissertations. Because independent research is encouraged and expected of faculty members, facilities and time for individual projects are generally available and both institutional and external funding for research are more typically accessible. The doctorate or an appropriate terminal degree is generally required.

Institutions Granting Baccalaureates as the Highest Degree. Faculty members may be responsible for upper- or lower-division courses, honors seminars, or supervision of independent study. Independent research may be encouraged, but greater emphasis is usually placed upon classroom instruction. Terminal degrees are preferred but some opportunities exist at the master's level.

Institutions Granting Associates as the Highest Degree. Faculty members are responsible for instruction of students in two-year associate degree programs. Programs may be terminal or designed as lower-division courses for students who transfer to institutions awarding baccalaureate degrees. Most often, classroom teaching is emphasized and a master's degree is usually a minimum requirement for employment.

Institutions Granting Certificates and Diplomas. Faculty members teach courses directly related to a trade or vocation. Classroom instruction and supervision of on-site learning experiences are typical responsibilities. Programs lead to a certificate or diploma rather than an academic degree. A bachelor's degree is usually the minimum requirement for employment.

College Preparatory Schools. Faculty and staff are hired to teach classes, to counsel students regarding academic and personal matters, and to provide specialized services. It is not unusual for faculty members in preparatory schools to hold advanced degrees. In many states, preparatory school teachers need not obtain teaching certificates required for teachers in public schools. Individuals who want to pursue elementary or secondary teaching should consult the book *From Contract to Contract: A Teacher's Employment Guide* (Anthony and Roe, Carroll Press) for a complete discussion of appropriate job-seeking strategies and techniques.

PROFESSIONAL OPPORTUNITIES

Academic institutions also offer employment opportunities in the form of a variety of professional staff positions. Positions can range from entry-level assignments to top-level administrative posts. The size of the institution determines the number of staff members and the administrative hierarchy. For example, a small college may employ only one professional staff member in its financial aid office, while a large university may employ a director of financial aid, an associate director, one or more assistant directors, and several junior staff members in entry-level positions.

Community-based organizations may operate in a similar fashion. A local museum may employ only one person to handle all curatorial and administrative responsibilities. On the other hand, a very large, multifaceted institution such as Chicago's Field Museum of Natural History employs a great number of professionals in departments ranging from archaeological studies to zoological exhibits. As a general rule, entry-level positions at larger organizations allow much greater specialization; at smaller organizations the duties and responsibilities tend to be more comprehensive. Each setting offers possibilities for advancement either within the institution or as a stepping-stone to another organization.

Employment opportunities for Ph.D.'s and M.A.'s exist in local, state, and federal government agencies. Typical jobs for persons with advanced degrees include positions as researchers, analysts, librarians, communications specialists, illustrators, and trainers. State and federal agencies usually offer entry-level positions with the opportunity to advance or transfer to midlevel or even higher classifications in management and administration. Positions may become available at any time during the year, and many federal agencies hire from occupational registers compiled by the Office of Personnel Management. However, agencies such as the Library of Congress, the Federal Bureau of Investigation, the Central Intelligence Agency, and the National Security Agency should be contacted directly for application information. For information about application procedures for state and federal government positions, contact the Federal Job Information Center or the state job service office nearest you.

INTERNATIONAL OPPORTUNITIES

Colleges and universities in virtually every part of the world employ American or American-educated faculty and administrators. Faculty members may be recruited for permanent positions or for short-term appointments. Academics and other professionals can consider careers in foreign affairs and international service organizations. Employers include the United States government, consulting firms, research organizations, nonprofit and charitable foundations, and international commissions.

Seeking a position in a foreign country will require some modification of job-search strategies and techniques. *Educators' Passport to International Jobs* (Anthony and Roe, Peterson's Guides) outlines application procedures, illustrates the preparation of a vita or résumé appropriate to foreign employment, provides insiders' tips on interview techniques, and offers suggestions for adapting to a new country. Other books of interest are: *Careers in International Affairs* (School of Foreign Service, Georgetown University), *The Overseas List* (Augsburg Publishing House), and *Americans Abroad* (Praeger Publishers).

FINDING WHAT'S AVAILABLE

After you have determined the scope of your job search, including the types of positions and the geographic locations you will consider, you can begin to look for announcements of available positions for which you can apply. Academic and professional positions are advertised through professional publications, journals, and newsletters. All academics should be familiar with *The Chronicle of Higher Education,* a weekly newspaper devoted to issues in postsecondary education, which contains the most comprehensive collection of faculty and administrative job announcements. Job seekers should also be aware that professional associations in most disciplines also publish job announcements; for example, the Modern Language Association publishes the *Job List* four times during the academic year. *Science,* a monthly publication, carries announcements of faculty and research positions in several scientific areas. Other publications announce both faculty and professional positions in many fields. The *Affirmative Action Register,* a monthly publication intended for women and minorities, covers faculty, professional, and managerial positions. A bimonthly publication, the *National Arts Jobbank,* lists faculty positions as well as announcements for various other jobs in the visual and performing arts. Some publications focus on specific types of opportunities, such as *Community Jobs,* a monthly publication carrying articles and announcements of internships and jobs in nonprofit community organizations throughout the United States, and *Federal Jobs,* a biweekly listing of job openings with the federal government.

All these publications can be obtained on a subscription basis. If you are on campus, however, you can check with your department, the college placement office, and college or departmental libraries to see if the publications are already available. In addition to published vacancies, your department may receive letters from academic institutions and other organizations announcing available positions. Check with your department to determine if current job notices are routinely posted on a bulletin board or filed in job notebooks. Campus placement offices also receive job announcements which may be posted or listed in vacancy bulletins.

WHAT TO LOOK FOR IN A JOB ANNOUNCEMENT

Available positions may be announced by individual departments or through a central office such as Personnel, Affirmative Action, Academic Affairs, or even the President's Office. In addition to the specific description of the available position, announcements disseminated by a designated central office are more likely to contain additional information about the institution, its special programs and accreditation, and the community. Job descriptions can be written by the department head, faculty or staff members, a search committee, or a personnel officer. As a general rule, the most complete job descriptions are written by the people closest to the position to be filled.

Because positions are now widely advertised through various publications and professional journals, the job seeker has access to considerable information about the number and variety of positions available throughout the country. A direct result of the widespread advertising of vacancies is increased competition for available positions, at least in terms of the number of applications submitted. For this reason, it is essential to read the vacancy notice carefully so that you can determine your interest in the opening, tailor your application materials to fit the duties and responsibilities of the position, and also be assured that you follow exactly the application procedures specified by the employing institution. Important items to look for in any job announcement include:

Title/level of position. Academics and professionals must look beyond the job title or rank to determine their eligibility for an available position. In addition to the familiar ranks of instructor, assistant professor, associate professor, and professor, other common academic titles include lecturer, researcher, fellow, visiting professor, artist or writer in residence, etc. Ranks and titles are established by guidelines covering qualifications, previous experiences, and descriptions of performance requirements. Definitions of positions and titles are not universally agreed upon; for example, the title of lecturer may define an entry-level position at one institution and a temporary but senior-level position at another. Some colleges do not assign professorial rank; beginning and experienced faculty members share the same title. As a general rule, however, first-time job seekers will be considered for entry-level positions carrying the title of instructor or assistant professor. Faculty positions above the entry level usually carry the title of associate professor or professor. To receive serious consideration for these senior positions, the applicant must hold an equivalent rank or have an outstanding record of achievement in a position of lower rank.

Similarly, titles for nonacademic employment in social service agencies, clinics, hospitals, libraries, and state or federal government departments and offices may vary greatly and are not necessarily indicative of the nature of the duties and responsibilities assigned. Do not rule out any job possibility simply on the basis of the title.

Term of appointment. If the vacancy notice does not indicate anything about the term or duration of the announced position, you can usually assume that it is intended to be a continuing or permanent appointment. In cases where the position is temporary, the vacancy appointment should include such phrases as "one-year replacement position," "sabbatical replacement," "three-year, fixed-term appointment" or even "contingent upon continued funding." For most academics the most desirable or sought-after positions are those that offer the possibility of a permanent appointment or continuing contract, often designated as "tenure-track" positions. Recently, budget constraints and other restrictions have reduced the number of positions advertised as tenure-track. Many positions are advertised as fixed-term appointments ranging in duration from one to three years. Some of these positions may be renewable and some may ultimately lead to tenure-track appointments. To obtain tenure, an academic must meet the criteria established by the institution within a specified number of years. Traditionally, tenure has been awarded to those who demonstrate excellence in teaching, research, and academic or community service. Today, tenure considerations may also include the individual's national or even international reputation as a scholar or leader in the field. Recognition is usually attained through significant publication or, in the arts, through a significant record of performances or commissions.

Most academics and professionals do not really expect to retire from the institution which offers them their first appointment, yet some job seekers make the mistake of limiting their applications only to those positions which offer the possibility of employment for an entire career. There are obvious advantages to applying for positions which offer at least the possibility of permanence, but the job seeker who is determined to apply only for permanent or continuing positions will usually find fewer opportunities. Comparatively few people really enjoy the prospect of relocating every year or two, but if it is at all feasible to consider temporary appointments it is generally professionally advantageous to do so. Obtaining your next position is usually easier after you have been employed in your profession even on a temporary basis. It would be mistakenly optimistic to expect that a one-year replacement position will become permanent, but this, too, can happen. In any event, the experience gained in a temporary appointment will be a positive factor in future job searches. Even a one-year position offers concrete, demonstrable evidence that you are employable.

Responsibilities and duties. Some vacancy notices are very specific about the exact duties and responsibilities of the available position. Others may give only a brief overview of the nature of the job, and some may list only the title of the position. Use the information presented to your best advantage. Focus your application on the experiences and training that qualify you to perform the required tasks or assume the stated responsibilities. If information is sketchy, you will usually need to present yourself as a generalist and emphasize your strongest capabilities. Bear in mind that the position description may represent a broader range of responsibilities than any one individual will be expected to assume. Adjustments in the exact nature of the duties may be made after applications have been reviewed. It is not worth your time or effort to apply for jobs for which you are obviously not qualified, but if you are qualified for the major portion of the described responsibilities and hold the required degree or its equivalent, you should consider submitting your application.

Accreditation. Announcements may include information about institutional or program accreditation. Accreditation ensures that the institutions follows established guidelines and developed objectives for instructional programs, maintains adequate facilities to support learning experiences, and continuously reviews achievements and goals. Eight regional nongovernmental associations (see Appendix for names and regions) evaluate and approve institutional accreditation according to established criteria. In addition to accreditation for institutions, programs offered by individual departments or colleges of a university may be accredited by professional associations such as the Accrediting Commission on Education for Health Services, the National Association of Schools of Music, Accreditation Board for Engineering and Technology, etc. Institutions and professional programs are reviewed on a regular basis and accreditation may be renewed upon recommendation or denied if appropriate standards are not maintained.

Required or preferred qualifications. When positions are announced or advertised, exact degree requirements may be specified. The terms for advanced degrees differ somewhat from one institution to another and the variations are often reflected in vacancy announcements. Typical master's degree designations include Master of Arts (M.A.), Master of Science (M.S.), Master of Social Work (M.S.W.), Master of Library Science (M.L.S.), Master of Business Administration (M.B.A.), and Master of Arts in Teaching (M.A.T.). Intermediate degrees representing work beyond the master's level but below the doctorate may include Master of Fine Arts (M.F.A.) and Education Specialist (Ed.S.). The most common designations for academic doctorates are Doctor of Philosophy (Ph.D.), Doctor of Education (Ed.D.), Doctor of Arts (D.A.), Doctor of Fine Arts (D.F.A.), and Doctor of Musical Arts (D.M.A.).

It is not unusual for an announcement to state that a terminal degree or its equivalent is required or preferred. In most fields the master's degree is not considered a terminal degree. The M.F.A. in the visual and performing arts and the doctorate in any field are considered terminal degrees. Thus, if an advertisement stated "terminal degree required," both M.F.A.'s and doctorates could be considered. If an announcement stated "M.F.A. required," a person holding an appropriate doctorate could apply, but the reverse would not be true.

Requirements or preferences for experience may also be stated. Inexperienced people can apply for positions if an announcement states only that experience is preferred. If an announcement indicates that experience is necessary ("minimum of one to two years' experience required"), you will probably not be considered unless you can demonstrate at least the equivalent of the stated requirement. Concentrate your energies on applying for positions for which you meet or exceed the stated minimum requirements.

Starting date. Almost all vacancy announcements for jobs in academic settings, whether for faculty or staff positions, will indicate a starting date. The starting dates for teaching positions are rarely negotiable; unless you will be available at the specified time your application may simply be a waste of time regardless of your qualifications. Research or support staff positions can allow some latitude or flexibility, and starting dates are often indicated as, for example, "January 1 or as soon as possible thereafter." If no starting date is indicated, you can submit your application indicating the earliest date you could be available. The employer may be able to adjust the starting date to accommodate the candidate who appears best qualified.

Application deadline. Pay careful attention to stated deadlines for submitting application materials. Some announcements clearly indicate that all materials (letter, vita, dossier, portfolio) must be received or postmarked by a given date; others may simply indicate a closing date with no specific instructions. In such cases, your letter of application and vita may suffice and supplemental materials can be submitted later. Follow directions carefully and make every effort to comply with the employer's request. Missing a deadline may not only put you at a disadvantage—it may completely eliminate your application from consideration.

Salary. Salary information on a vacancy announcement can be exact ($26,000), approximate (salary range: $22,000 to $28,000, or minimum salary $22,000), or ambiguous (negotiable, or commensurate with qualifications and experience). Employers can choose to state salary information in one of these three ways depending upon the level of the position, the available funding, and the amount of latitude they may have to negotiate starting salary. Some employers have little or no latitude because of contractual provisions regarding salary schedules. Others can select the best person for the position and then meet salary expectations or requirements. Always be ready to negotiate, but be prepared for the fact that the employer may not be able to do so.

TAPPING SOURCES OF SUPPORT

Although you must take personal responsibility for initiating and conducting an effective job search, you should not overlook the assistance that may be available from mentors, placement counselors, and colleagues or peers. These individuals can often offer advice and support to help you through the various stages of your job search and can be of invaluable assistance in helping you arrive at sound decisions about employment opportunities.

MENTORS

Mentors not only play an important role in graduate education, guiding their students through the complexities of a degree program, the anxieties of comprehensive examinations, and the proposal, research, and writing of a thesis or dissertation; they also can be instrumental in helping students launch their careers. Certainly the mentor's appraisal of a graduate is valued by potential employers because the close, intensive relationship between mentor and student enables the mentor to assess performance, character, and potential. Perhaps no other person can make so accurate a prediction of what a student will be like as a colleague and as a professional. Mentors traditionally function as sounding boards and motivators for students who are about to leave the fold; their experiences, sometimes with generations of students, and their knowledge of the field and the opportunities it can afford can be enormously helpful to the new job seeker.

PLACEMENT COUNSELORS

A source of support that is sometimes overlooked by graduate students and alumni is the campus placement office. In most cases, a placement counselor will be able to identify with your situation, listen to your concerns, and perhaps offer constructive advice to help you gain a perspective on your situation. Placement counselors, because of the nature of their relationship with students and alumni, can often be more objective than a mentor or academic adviser with whom a close personal relationship has been established during the course of your graduate study. A placement counselor can reassure you that you are conducting your job search effectively and confirm that your expectations are realistic or offer advice for modifications.

PEERS

Another source of support may develop naturally if you are in regular contact with other people who share your employment objectives. In a large department there may be several graduate students who, like yourself, are in the process of seeking jobs. Your common interests, shared experiences, and similar goals make it easy to share your thoughts, your concerns, and your frustrations with each other. If you are in a small department, it may be possible to form a support group composed of graduate students from several different disciplines.

Whether your group develops naturally within your own department or you make the effort to bring in other people, a good support group can help you to maintain your enthusiasm, perspective, and sense of purpose during the high and low points of a job search. One of the most useful functions of a support group is to help each member examine attitudes that can pose obstacles to a successful job search. Some job seekers are defeated before they even begin because they overemphasize the difficulties and barriers. Some may use the market as an excuse. But no matter how intense the competition may be, the only sure way not to get a job is not to apply for any. The support group can help you to realize that your search is not a hopeless cause and can provide the necessary motivation to keep you from giving up. In addition, a support group can help you to work through some other defeatist attitudes that can be summarized as:

- Somebody else is a "shoo-in"
- I'm not good enough/I'm too good
- I'm outside the network

In certain circumstances these attitudes may appear valid, but not in all cases. Let's take a closer look at them.

SOMEBODY ELSE IS A "SHOO-IN"

Thousands of academic and professional positions are advertised each year, and it is true that some of these positions are "wired"—that is, they are advertised in compliance with state and federal hiring guidelines but the person who will fill the position may have been selected even before the position is announced. These situations can result from promotions from within or the creation of a position to allow a person already on staff to use special skills and talents, or they may result from nepotism or some other form of favoritism. The job descriptions written for these positions may offer some clues, but it is usually not possible, without direct inside information, to determine whether a particular position will be filled on an open and competitive basis. One should never assume that the position is not available to the best-qualified candidate.

I'M NOT GOOD ENOUGH/I'M TOO GOOD

It is no secret that academic snobbery exists. The prestige and reputation of the department and institution advertising a vacancy as well as the influence and renown of the department and institution granting your degree can be factors in the selection process. Some institutions traditionally hire graduates of certain types of colleges and universities. This is a simple fact and it is an employment practice that is not without justification in many instances. But do not assume that you cannot apply for a position simply because you did not attend an institution of comparable rank and stature. Do not fall victim to the misconception that having a degree from a less prestigious institution automatically closes off opportunities at better-known institutions or the reverse—that having a degree from a prestigious school eliminates potential job opportunities at lesser-known institutions. Never assume that no options exist for "outsiders." If the job is appealing and you meet the stated requirements, you should submit your application presenting yourself as advantageously as possible, and allow your qualifications to speak for themselves. Search committees may be more broad-minded than you imagine, but if you allow your biases and prejudices to prevent you from applying, you may never have the chance to expand your opportunities.

I'M OUTSIDE THE NETWORK

The old-boy network has a long tradition in academic and professional circles and will undoubtedly remain influential as long as humans are responsible for hiring. While there is no denying that old-boy and new-woman networks have a place in the selection process, their importance and power may be exaggerated. Influential friends can certainly be of assistance to a job seeker, but the idea that you do not stand a chance without a substantial network behind you is a myth. A network is only as effective or as good as the people in it. Complicated networks must be used judiciously, because if any one contact is not reliable, respected, or trustworthy the networking process can fail or even backfire. Useful as networks can be, time should not be wasted in attempting to create a network where none exists, nor should one depend upon contacts and networks for every application. Not even the most complex network or influential contact can eliminate the various steps involved in an academic or professional job search.

GAINING PROFESSIONAL RECOGNITION

Regardless of the assistance that can be provided by mentors, placement counselors, or support groups, the responsibility for each stage of a successful job search is yours alone. You are the only one who can take control of your job search and you are the only one who can maximize your chances for success. Perhaps the most obvious method of promoting yourself is to gain recognition by participating in professional activities.

Almost without exception, applicants for academic posts will be expected to show evidence of their ability to contribute to the body of knowledge in their discipline. "Publish or perish" is a phrase that has been in almost constant use among people in academe for a good many years, but the phrase may be even more prophetic today than it has ever been. Either in written recommendations or in direct conversation with potential employers, your mentor and principal teachers can promote your candidacy by stressing your writing abilities and their expectations that you will prove to be a productive professional.

Very few people at the beginning of their career will have published extensively, but the doctoral dissertation or master's thesis can demonstrate potential for scholarly writing. If you have published articles or book reviews, particularly in professional or refereed journals, of course you will want to ensure that prospective employers are aware of these publications and you should be prepared to provide offprints or copies of the material.

Although publishing can almost be considered essential for a successful academic career, it can also be important for professionals in any field. Even if publishing is not a criterion for selection or promotion in nonacademic jobs, professional writing is an asset because it promotes credibility and demonstrates a commitment to the profession. Whether or not it is imperative that you publish, publications will make you more competitive for jobs in your field. In addition to enhancing your employment prospects, writing for publication allows you to contribute to your profession and to realize personal and professional goals.

Participation in professional conferences is another way to increase your chances for employment. Most professional associations regularly invite advanced graduate students as well as faculty members or practitioners to submit proposals for presentations of papers or workshops. Participation in a professional conference can be an honor, but—even more important for a job seeker—it affords the opportunity for visibility and recognition from colleagues, peers, and potential employers. Although presenting a paper or leading a workshop session can give you optimal visibility, there are other ways to gain exposure. You could volunteer to serve as recorder for a session, facilitator for a panel, reactor for an address by a featured speaker, or member of a planning committee. Recognition can also be gained through "behind the scenes" activities. Nearly all associations have established standing committees dealing with such items as membership, publications and communications, research, constitution and by-laws, and professional growth and development. Your work as a committee member can bring you into contact with individuals in your field and help to establish your reputation as an ambitious, responsible, and committed professional. Through active participation in academic and professional associations, graduate students, junior faculty, or professionals in the early stages of their careers can gain personal recognition and professional benefits.

PREPARING TO MARKET YOURSELF

Marketing yourself to potential employers will be much easier if you have taken the time to organize and develop strategies for an effective job search. Once you have determined that you have the commitment, the time, and the resources to initiate and carry through a job search, you can identify possible employers and people who can help you through the initial stages of the selection process and activities that will promote your candidacy. When the organizational stage is accomplished, you can turn your attention to the tools and techniques you will need to communicate your skills and qualifications to potential employers.

Chapter Two

The Vita and the Résumé—
Variations on a Theme

By the time you start looking for professional employment, you will undoubtedly know that you need to prepare either a résumé or a *curriculum vitae,* also known as a vita, or c.v. (While it is true that vita is in a different Latin form than vitae, causing some to say that it cannot be used as a shortened term for *curriculum vitae,* it can be seen as an alternative, equally valid, term for the document, i.e., "[my] life." In any case, the term is certainly here to stay, and we will use it throughout our discussion.)

If you are like most job seekers, you have some idea of what a résumé is, but you may be uncertain about the definition and purpose of a vita. Simply speaking, a résumé summarizes educational preparation and experience and may legitimately include any experience relevant to one's career objective. The academic community's preferred vita concentrates on academic pursuits and omits all material not directly related to educational background and achievement. In other words, a vita is prepared for academic pursuits; a résumé is developed for other occupations. Whether a vita or a résumé is prepared depends upon professional background and career objective. Individuals exploring a variety of career options should prepare both a vita and a résumé.

The following pages discuss and illustrate the preparation and use of the résumé and vita in the job search and in career development. Without exception, anyone seeking a position in higher education or in various service professions must develop and use effectively one or both of these job-seeking tools. This chapter will answer questions and present ideas which will enable you to prepare these documents with understanding and confidence.

THE VERSATILE VITA

USING YOUR VITA IN THE EMPLOYMENT PROCESS

Understanding the various uses of the vita in the employment process is important for beginning job seekers and experienced professionals alike. As a first step in the process of applying for a position, it is customary to introduce yourself to a prospective employer by sending a copy of your vita with a cover letter. In some situations the vita can be presented without a cover letter. For example, it is appropriate to give a copy of your vita to potential employers you encounter at conferences or other professional meetings. Think of your vita as a detailed, oversized calling card. With or without an accompanying letter, the vita helps to create the vitally important first impression of you as a potential colleague. The better the first impression, the greater your chances of being selected for an interview.

If you are invited to interview for an academic or professional position, you may be interviewed by several people and you may even encounter group interview situations. Most of the people you talk with will have had the opportunity to review your vita, but it is always advisable to give each member of the committee a copy of your vita to facilitate interview questions. Providing a copy for each person involved in the selection process assures you that all parties are aware of your qualifications and also demonstrates your foresight and organizational skills.

Even before you submit your vita to a prospective employer it can assist you with your job search. Whether you request a written recommendation or simply the privilege of using a person's name as a reference, it will be to your advantage to provide a copy of your vita. No matter how unforgettable we may think we are, former—and even current—professional acquaintances cannot carry every important detail in their memories. The vita will help the individual to give accurate answers to inquiries from potential employers and will enable a written reference to focus on the strengths and experiences appropriate to your job objective.

USING YOUR VITA IN CAREER DEVELOPMENT

Although most people think of the vita primarily as a tool in the job search, it is a versatile and far-reaching statement. A vita is not discarded after an appointment has been accepted; it is a lifelong document. You begin accumulating vita information the day you enter college, and you will never write a final version; the vita grows and develops at all stages of your professional life from undergraduate student to professor emeritus. You may as well begin to think of your vita as a lifelong companion; it will be with you from now on—'til death do you part.

Among the many career stages and developments that call for presentation of a vita are:

- seeking a position
- departmental/tenure reviews
- campus and intercampus committee service
- professional association leadership
- speaking engagements
- publishing
- editorial review boards
- consulting
- grant applications
- sabbaticals
- fellowships

PREPARING AN EFFECTIVE VITA

The vita which represents you to prospective employers should not be prepared hastily, nor should you attempt to shortcut the process by delegating the responsibility to anyone else. Using a commercial résumé writer to produce the final version is usually not a satisfactory solution to the problem of creating an effective vita. The "middleman" cannot do your work for you; you still must take the responsibility for identifying and selecting items to be included, and you should not relinquish control of the material. You are the best judge of the sequence and weight of your carefully selected information. Allowing another person to produce your vita can result in an impersonal document which may look as if information had simply been plugged into prearranged categories.

As you begin to prepare your vita, you should be aware that the skeletal structure of any vita has three basic components: Identification (name and complete addresses), Education (degrees earned or in progress), and Professional Experience (current and previous work including graduate assistantships). Adding meat to the bare bones of the vita is not necessarily an easy task and your determination of the items to be included will require careful deliberation. Input from faculty members, a placement adviser, a colleague, or at least a fellow job seeker should be solicited. Any of these people may be able to spot inconsistencies, errors, or weaknesses. Consider their suggestions carefully, balance them against your convictions, and revise your vita to incorporate the suggestions that make sense to you. It is important to recognize that conflicting opinions of what is

CATEGORIES APPROPRIATE FOR THE VITA

Academic Preparation
Academic Training
Academic Background
Education
Educational Background
Educational Overview
Professional Studies
Degrees
Principal Teachers

Thesis
Master's Project
Comprehensive Areas
Dissertation
Dissertation Title

Professional Competencies
Educational Highlights
Course Highlights
Proficiencies
Areas of Knowledge
Areas of Expertise
Areas of Experience
Areas of Concentration in
    Graduate Study

Professional Experience
Professional Overview
Professional Background
Teaching Experience
Teaching Overview
Experience Summary
Experience Highlights
Research Experience
Research Overview
Administrative Experience
Consulting Experience
Continuing Education Experience
Related Experience

Internships
Teaching/Research Assistantships
Graduate Fieldwork
Graduate Practica

Academic Accomplishments
Professional Achievements
Career Achievements
Career Highlights
Background

Publications
Scholarly Publications
Scholarly Works
Books
Professional Papers
Articles/Monographs
Reviews
Exhibits/Exhibitions
Arrangements/Scores

Academic Service
Professional Service
University Involvement
Service
Faculty Leadership
Committee Leadership
Departmental Leadership
Professional Association Leadership
    and Activities

Scholarly Presentations
Conference Presentations
Convention Addresses
Workshop Presentations
Workshops and Conventions
Programs and Workshops
Conferences Attended
Conference Participation
Conference Leadership

Memberships
Affiliations
Professional Memberships
Memberships in Scholarly Societies
Professional Organizations

Professional Certification
Certificates
Licensure
Special Training
Endorsements

Teaching Interests
Academic Interests
Research Interests
Educational Interests
Professional Interests

Scholarships
Fellowships
Academic Awards
Special Honors
Distinctions
College Distinctions
Activities and Distinctions
Honors and Distinctions
Honors and Awards
Prizes
College Activities

Foreign Study
Study Abroad
Travel Abroad
Languages
Language Competencies

Dossier
Credentials
Placement File
References
Recommendations

necessary and desirable will be offered by well-meaning friends and associates, but not every fact about your personal and professional life belongs on a vita. The following lists of suggested vita and résumé categories can serve as a useful starting point by assisting you with the identification of appropriate elements to cover in each document and by suggesting a variety of terms which can be used to classify and arrange items of interest to potential employers.

WHAT ABOUT A RÉSUMÉ?

Job seekers who are considering positions other than collegiate faculty or research appointments will often benefit from preparing a résumé. Résumés are typically used for positions in business but are also effective for certain types of positions within the academic community, especially in the areas of student services and administration. The résumé may include categories from the vita list as well as some of the headings from the résumé categories list.

CATEGORIES APPROPRIATE FOR THE RÉSUMÉ

Objective	Writing Skills
Job Objective	Speaking Skills
Employment Objective	Leadership Skills
Career Objective	Organizational Skills
Professional Objective	Administrative Skills
Position Desired	Technical Skills
Current Employment	Volunteer Activities
Employment	Related Activities
Employment Record	Civic Activities
Other Work	Community Involvement
Part-Time Work	Community and Other Activities
Summer Work Experience	Special Talents
Additional Experience	Leisure Activities
Special Skills	Interests
Research Skills	Personal Interests
Design and Development Skills	Military Service
Computer Skills	

PERSONAL INFORMATION

The suggested category headings listed above concentrate on appropriate professional and related activities and interests. There are some employers who want to know your age, marital status, and number of dependents, but we contend that these and other personal characteristics are not relevant—and federal legislation agrees with us. Tell them what they need to know, not necessarily everything they want to know. Certain information cannot be requested and need not be offered. Age, sex, race, religion, national origin, and height and weight should not be of consequence in the selection process. Don't make the mistake of letting a committee member or potential employer discount your application because of a personal bias. Think about your reasons for preparing and submitting a vita. You are trying to obtain a position which will allow you to use your professional qualifications—not to win a beauty or popularity contest.

Although personal information is not appropriate on a vita, many institutions will request that you complete an Affirmative Action form which specifies age, sex, race, and national origin. This form is not part of the application materials reviewed by the search committee. Although completion of this form is optional, the employing institution uses the data to report compliance with state equal employment opportunity guidelines and regulations established by the U.S. Equal Employment Opportunity Commission and the Office of Civil Rights in the Department of Education. A typical Affirmative Action form will probably resemble the sample shown here.

LONG OR SHORT?

You have probably heard or read that a résumé must be limited to a single page. While employers in the business world may prefer a rather standard one-page résumé, academics and professionals applying for jobs in other settings should not be unduly concerned about the length of the vita nor feel obligated to conform to the restrictions of the business world. Don't panic if the first draft is depressingly short or alarmingly long. Put it away for a while and when you come to revise it you may well find significant items that need to be added or extraneous material that can be easily removed.

Within reason, the content of your vita—not the academic degree you hold, the amount of experience, or any arbitrary rule—will determine its length. It is not true that a Ph.D. must have a longer, more detailed vita than a person with a master's degree. The quality and relevance of the information is more significant than the total number of pages filled. Remember, a vita is neither a narrative nor an outline. Only items pertinent to your objective deserve a place, but they must be developed in sufficient detail to convey the importance of the information.

Rather than fretting about the number of pages, concentrate on producing a vita that is sufficiently detailed but concisely written. Experienced professionals, unlike beginners, may require more than one or two pages to convey information relevant to their qualifications. Individuals with extensive publications, profes-

SAMPLE FORM

CENTRAL STATE UNIVERSITY
EQUAL EMPLOYMENT OPPORTUNITY INFORMATION

Information from this form will be held confidential and will be used only to facilitate the reporting and auditing of affirmative action progress at Central State University. This form will not be filed with other application materials and will not be considered in the selection process.

Although completion of this form is voluntary, your cooperation is requested. Any information not provided by the applicant will be supplied by the University on a "best knowledge" basis as required by legal compliance with equal employment opportunity regulations.

NAME: _____
       last   first   middle   maiden

AGE: _____ SEX: ☐MALE ☐FEMALE U.S. CITIZEN: ☐YES ☐NO

VETERAN: ☐YES ☐NO If yes, discharge date _____.

HANDICAP: ☐YES ☐NO If yes, cite handicap and any special work limitations below:

_____

RACE OR ETHNIC BACKGROUND. Check one.

☐ AMERICAN INDIAN OR ALASKAN NATIVE (persons having origins in any of the original peoples of North America and who maintain cultural identification through tribal affiliation or community recognition).

☐ ASIAN OR PACIFIC ISLANDER (persons having origins in any of the original peoples of the Far East, Southeast Asia, the Indian Subcontinent, or the Pacific Islands).

☐ BLACK (persons having origins in any of the Black racial groups of Africa).

☐ HISPANIC (persons of Mexican, Puerto Rican, Cuban, Central or South American origin).

☐ WHITE (persons having origins in any of the original peoples of Europe, North Africa, or the Middle East).

WHAT IS THE POSITION FOR WHICH YOU ARE APPLYING? State exact title below:

_____

HOW DID YOU LEARN OF THE POSITION?

☐ Central State University personnel office.
☐ Central State University job announcement. Where? _____
☐ Professional journal or newspaper advertisement. Publication? _____
☐ Referred by employment agency or placement office. Name? _____
☐ Referred by present or former employee of Central State University.
☐ Referred by friend or relative.
☐ Other; explain: _____

_____

sional activities, or performances will find that this material can be effectively and advantageously organized and presented in an achievements or accomplishments section covering these basic components: identification, education, and professional experience. Two samples at the end of this chapter illustrate the use of a professional achievements page, which could be expanded to several pages if necessary.

The net result of this approach is to streamline the vita into two distinct but equally important parts. The writer benefits because the material is more easily organized and updates and revisions can be accomplished with a minimum of effort and expense. The reader also benefits from this approach because an overview can be obtained quickly; extensive documentation of professional activities can be closely examined without breaking the reader's train of thought. As you know, the vita is only one of many items reviewed by the search committee. Aside from their regular teaching or administrative duties, committee members are inundated with stacks and stacks of vitas, letters, transcripts, dossiers, and portfolios. Submitting a concise, well-written vita will maximize your chances of having it read with proper attention from beginning to end.

PREPARING MORE THAN ONE VERSION OF YOUR VITA

If you are willing to consider positions in a variety of settings, preparing alternate versions of your vita allows you to emphasize strengths, experiences, and educational background most appropriate to each setting. Because institutions vary in their mission, goals, and objectives, the emphasis you place on your experiences in research or teaching can influence the action of a search committee. For example, a community college search committee will be more favorably impressed with a vita focusing on teaching interests and skills than on research or related activities. For institutions where teaching will be a primary consideration, especially in two-year colleges,

STRESS

- teaching experience
- teaching interests
- qualifications as a generalist
- courses or certificates applicable to community colleges
- attendance at community colleges
- student contact (especially with lower-division students)

27

DO NOT STRESS

- research experience
- research interests
- graduate specialization
- thesis or dissertation topics

Whatever type of position you are seeking, you should be aware that two versions of your vita may be essential for use at professional conferences. If the conference offers a placement service which allows employers to review a job seeker's vita, limitations may be placed on the number of vita pages. Most often, two pages are maximum. Since in all probability additional pages will simply be discarded, don't exceed the stipulated number of pages—even if it means writing a new vita. You can always present your more detailed version to any employer who expresses interest and contacts you on the basis of the vita submitted to the placement service.

There is always the chance that informal conversations on the conference floor, at receptions, or even in elevators will develop into serious discussions of employment possibilities. Be prepared—have extra copies of your vita on hand. If you are caught off-guard and empty-handed, indicate to the potential employer that a vita can be delivered to the hotel desk or sent via U.S. mail. Even if you have given a potential employer a copy of your vita at a conference, always follow up with a letter and another copy of the vita after returning home. In the flurry of conference activities your vita could be misplaced and lost forever.

PRODUCING AN ATTRACTIVE VITA

Employers expect to receive attractive, interesting, and flawless vitas. Whether you are preparing one version of your vita or several, it is important to understand that there may be any number of acceptable styles and formats, but there are only three cardinal rules.

- Your vita must be accurate and current.

  The vita loses its value if the material presented is incorrect or out-of-date. Pay careful attention to dates, names, and descriptions in all entries. All items may be subject to inquiry and must be verifiable. Never send an outdated vita. There are two options if the vita is not ready when an opening is announced. Either delay the application until the vita is ready or send a letter of application without a vita if the deadline is imminent. Under no circumstances make handwritten additions, corrections, or comments on the vita you send to employers.

- Your vita must be error free.

  You've heard this before and you'll hear it again—proofread, proofread, proofread. Don't expect perfection of a typist or printer, and don't count on them to catch your mistakes. Errors in spelling or grammar create an unnecessary and undesirable interruption for the reader and may raise questions about your attention to detail and your writing abilities.

- Your vita must be visually pleasing.

  Before the reader has a chance to examine the content of the vita, first impressions have already been made. The look and feel of the paper, agreeable typeface, sufficient margins, and adequate white space all contribute to a favorable first impression. Calculate the amount of material to be included, consider the various category designations, and then create or design a format that accents your academic and professional background and presents a visual image worthy of the content.

METHODS OF PRODUCTION

Mechanical duplication of your vita should never be considered. Carbon paper, spirit masters, and mimeograph stencils cannot produce the crisp, clear image essential for a professional appearance. For best results, the vita should be either typeset or photographically reproduced on good quality bond paper. Avoid printing on both sides of the page, odd-size paper, script or gothic lettering, and gimmicks (unusual folding, bright colors, strange or whimsical graphics).

A professionally typeset vita is possibly the most attractive and certainly the most expensive, but there are several advantages and disadvantages to be considered.

The advantages of professional typesetting include:

- It's easy. All supplies are in one location and only one person needs to be consulted.

- A good typewriter and expert typing are not required. The printer can work from a handwritten copy if it is legible and without errors.

- Various typefaces can be used throughout the vita for emphasis and effect.

- Copies will be attractive, clear, and easy to read.

- A wide choice of paper quality and color is available for the vita and for letters and envelopes.

Disadvantages include:

- Appearance may be too slick.
- Cost could be prohibitive.

- Turnaround time could be lengthy due to setup time and necessity of checking proofs.

- Reruns are expensive.

- Updates and alterations cost money.

Multilith or offset printing is a photographic process available to students, faculty, and staff members on many campuses through campus copy centers or commercial outlets. This process, like the typeset process, has several pros and cons.

The advantages of multilith include:

- It's inexpensive. Copies can be reproduced at a fraction of the cost of typesetting.

The disadvantages include:

- May require a professional typist. Originals cannot be prepared on erasable paper because shadows will appear on the finished copy. Placement of items on the page requires good typing skills.

- Preparing the original can be time-consuming. A balanced appearance on the finished product may require several drafts.

- Limited choice of typeface allows less opportunity for variation to create emphasis or visual attractiveness.

Whichever method you choose for reproducing your vita, don't settle for anything less than a good, dark, clear copy on quality paper. Whether the vita is typeset or photographically reproduced, you are responsible for its appearance. Very simply, if the vita doesn't look good, you don't look good. Because it usually serves to introduce you to the employer, it is vitally important that the content and the appearance of the vita contribute to the professional profile you want to convey.

CHOOSING A FORMAT THAT SUITS YOUR CURRENT NEEDS

The ability to use a vita effectively and to your best advantage is a skill to be mastered; it is not automatically acquired with age, rank, or status. In the course of your career you will prepare multiple versions of your vita, revising it to reflect your current situation. Whether it is used in a job search or in career development, the basic purpose remains: to convey information about your professional background and accomplishments. Before constructing your vita or résumé, study the samples on the following pages, which illustrate different styles, category designations, and ways of organizing and presenting information. Keep in mind that style and format are not necessarily linked to the discipline represented, and notice that it is the content, not the overall appearance, that distinguishes a vita from a résumé.

SAMPLE VITA—LITERATURE

CHRISTOPHER J. ASCHE

ADDRESSES

Home: 421 Walnut
      Tempe, Arizona 85281
      (602) 248-3001

Office: 3121 Communications Center
      Arizona State University
      Tempe, Arizona 85281
      (602) 248-1782

ACADEMIC TRAINING

Hiram College Hiram, Ohio	1974–1978	B.A. cum laude	English
The Ohio State University Columbus, Ohio	1978–1979	M.A.	English
Arizona State University Tempe, Arizona	1979–	Ph.D.	English
Cambridge University Cambridge, England	1981–1982		Elizabethan/Jacobean Drama

Comprehensive areas include: Renaissance Literature, 18th Century British Literature, Expository Writing.

Dissertation Title: Aesthetic Distance in the Early Comedies of Ben Jonson.

TEACHING AND RESEARCH EXPERIENCE

Teaching Assistant, Communications Program, Arizona State University, 1979–1981 Complete responsibility for instruction and grading of a two-semester freshman course stressing development of oral and written communication skills.

Research Assistant, Arizona State University, 1982–1983
Assisted Professors Gould and Perry in a review of the literature for a federally funded grant to implement a program in expository writing.

AWARDS AND DISTINCTIONS

Dean's List, Hiram College, 1974–1978
Homeier Senior Scholarship, Hiram College, 1977–1978
Who's Who in American Colleges, 1978
Representative, Arizona State University Student Senate, 1980–1981
The Robert Fay Literary Fellowship, 1981–1982
Student member, Departmental Advisory Committee, Arizona State University, 1979–present

PROFESSIONAL MEMBERSHIPS

Modern Language Association
Southwest Modern Language Association
Conference on College Composition and Communication

CONFERENCE PRESENTATION

"Myth and Fabliau: Sources for Jonson's *Volpone*," at the Southwest Modern Language Association Conference, Phoenix, Arizona, March, 1983

Complete dossier available from the Placement Center, McLean Hall, Arizona State University, Tempe, Arizona 85281   (602) 248-2022

SAMPLE VITA—CHEMISTRY

DENISE OVERMAN

ADDRESSES:	Home: 429 Oak Street Apt. #421B Lafayette, Indiana 47906 (317) 555-2664	Office: 204 Chemistry Building Purdue University West Lafayette, Indiana 47907 (317) 494-4000

EDUCATION:
1983 Ph.D., Purdue University, West Lafayette, Indiana
Physical Chemistry
Dissertation topic: Crystal structures of several intermetallic compounds of gadolinium and dyprosium with manganese and iron.
Dr. G. W. Terhune, adviser

1975 M.A., University of Minnesota, Minneapolis, Minnesota
Chemistry

1973 B.A., Cornell College, Mt. Vernon, Iowa
Chemistry/Physics

HONORS:
1981-83 National Science Foundation Fellow, Purdue Univ.
1974 John Upson Fellowship, University of Minnesota
1972-73 Martin-Merriwether Scholarship, Cornell College
1969-73 Dean's list (7 semesters), Cornell College

TEACHING EXPERIENCE:
1981-83 Teaching Assistant, Purdue University
General Chemistry, Physical Chemistry
1975-77 Chemistry Instructor, Augsburg College, Minneapolis, Minnesota

RELATED EXPERIENCE:
1977-79 Industrial Researcher, Monsanto Company, St. Louis, Missouri
1974 Summer Technical Assistant, 3M Company, St. Paul, Minnesota

TEACHING INTERESTS:
Undergraduate courses in physical and organic chemistry; graduate courses in physical chemistry

RESEARCH INTERESTS:
Determination of molecular structure of biologically important compounds using X-ray diffraction
Techniques of neutron diffraction

PUBLICATION:
"Structure of Uranium Dicarbide Determined by Neutron Diffraction," D. Overman and J. Hart, *Journal of Chemical Physics*, 42, 282, 1982.

MEMBERSHIPS:
Phi Beta Kappa
Alpha Chi Sigma
Phi Lambda Upsilon
American Chemical Society

SERVICE:
Departmental Undergraduate Curriculum Committee, 1981-82
Student Member, Search Committee for Dean of Graduate School, 1981
Secretary, Graduate Student Association, 1980-81

CREDENTIALS:
Educational Placement, Matthews Hall, Purdue University, West Lafayette, Indiana 47907 (317) 494-3990

SAMPLE VITA—MUSIC

RICHARD N. IVENDS

2244 Jackson Street
Seattle, Washington 98192
206/282-2163

ACADEMIC PREPARATION

Doctor of Musical Arts, University of Washington, Seattle, Washington, 1983
Master of Arts in Music, University of Oregon, Eugene, Oregon, 1975
Bachelor of Music, Seattle Pacific University, Seattle, Washington, 1973

PRINCIPAL TEACHERS

Choral Conducting: Robert Abrams   Voice: G. Todd Ziemann
                 Martin Maurer   Carroll Sunderman
                 John Warren   Lewine Naegele

EXPERIENCE

Acting Director of Choral Activities, Seattle Pacific University
     Seattle, Washington, 1982–83

         Replaced faculty member on sabbatical leave. Conducted Seattle Pacific
         University Chorus and Madrigal Singers, a select ensemble of 24 voices.

Graduate Assistant, Choral Conducting, University of Washington
     Seattle, Washington, 1980–82

         Conducted the University Chorale, a select ensemble of 32 voices; soloist,
         University of Washington Chorus, 1982

Assistant Professor, Choral Conducting and Voice, Linfield College
     McMinnville, Oregon, 1977–80

         Conducted Linfield College Choir, an ensemble of 80 voices, and Freshman
         Chorale, an ensemble of 36 voices. Taught private voice. Team taught a
         music appreciation course for freshmen and sophomores. Soloist, Linfield
         Faculty Quartet.

Director of Music, Plymouth Presbyterian Church, Portland, Oregon, 1975–77

         Conducted Senior Choir, an ensemble of 44 voices, and conducted Chapel
         Choir and Young People's Choir; soloist for services and special concerts.

PROFESSIONAL MEMBERSHIPS

American Choral Directors Association
College Music Society
Music Educators National Conference
National Association of Teachers of Singing

REFERENCES

Complete dossier available from University of Washington Placement Center,
301 Loew Hall, Seattle, Washington 98195

SAMPLE VITA—MUSIC

RICHARD N. IVENDS
Page 2

GUEST CONDUCTING EXPERIENCE

Oregon Community Chorus Festival, Portland, Oregon. June, 1983
Washington State High School Music Festival, Seattle, Washington. March, 1982
University of Washington Music Camp, Seattle, Washington. July, 1981
Oregon All-State Men's Chorus, Eugene, Oregon. February, 1981
University of Oregon Music Camp, Eugene, Oregon. July, 1980
Region XI Honors Choir, Medford, Oregon. April, 1980
Oregon High School Choral Clinic, Eugene, Oregon. March, 1979

MAJOR WORKS CONDUCTED

Bach	Cantata 6
	Cantata 120
	Cantata 146
	Motet 4
Brahms	Requiem
Fauré	Requiem
Handel	Messiah (excerpts)
Mozart	Regina Coeli, K.276
Orff	Carmina Burana (excerpts)
Saint-Saëns	Christmas Oratorio
Schubert	Mass in G
Williams	Dona Nobis Pacem
Vivaldi	Magnificat

REPRESENTATIVE PERFORMANCES AS VOCAL SOLOIST

Bach	B Minor Mass
	St. Matthew Passion
Handel	Messiah
Haydn	Harmoniemesse
Mendelssohn	Elijah
Mozart	Requiem
Stravinsky	Les Noces
Vivaldi	Gloria

SAMPLE VITA—STUDIO ART

BRENDAN MC CONNELL

ADDRESS:
1205 E. College
Des Moines, Iowa 50316

TELEPHONE:
(515) 281-3542 (Business)
(515) 286-2665 (Home)

TEACHING INTERESTS: Ceramics, Sculpture, 3-D Design, Graphics, Calligraphy

TEACHING EXPERIENCE:
Teaching Assistant, Iowa State University, Ceramics Studio, 1978–80
Sculpture Instructor, Drake University Union Craft Center, 1980–82
Ceramics Instructor, Des Moines Recreation Center, 1981–82

RELATED EXPERIENCE:
Matting and framing, Hogan's Art Supplies, Ames, part-time 1978–81
Own and operate ceramics studio and supply shop, 1982–present

JURIED SHOWS:
Upper Midwest Artists' Exhibition, Hamline University, St. Paul, Minnesota, 1977 (Student Award)
Mid-Mississippi Annual Exhibit, Davenport Art Center, Davenport, Iowa, 1978
30th Annual Iowa Artists' Exhibition, Des Moines Art Center, Des Moines, Iowa, 1980
St. Louis Ceramics Show, Mark Twain Gallery, St. Louis, Missouri, 1982 (Purchase Prize)

INVITATIONAL EXHIBITIONS:
Iowa Sculpture Invitational, The Blanden Gallery, Fort Dodge, Iowa, 1979
Contemporary Ceramics, The Cooper Gallery, Ames, Iowa, 1980

GROUP SHOWS:
Summer Art Show, Mount Mercy College, Cedar Rapids, Iowa, 1977
Graduate Student Exhibit, Iowa State University, Ames, Iowa, 1980
Sioux City Graphic Arts Show, Missouri Valley Art Center, Sioux City, Iowa, 1981

MEMBERSHIPS:
Midwest Sculptors' Association
College Art Association
Polk County Arts Council

DEGREES:
B.A. Studio Art, Drake University, Des Moines, Iowa, 1977
M.F.A. Studio Art, Iowa State University, Ames, Iowa, 1980

REFERENCES AVAILABLE UPON REQUEST

SAMPLE VITA—PHYSICAL EDUCATION

KARLA JOSEPH
1032 Elmhurst Avenue
Battle Creek, Michigan 49016
(606) 965-3802

PROFESSIONAL OBJECTIVE

Head Basketball Coach and Athletic Administrator

EXPERIENCE

1981–	Kellogg Community College, Battle Creek, Michigan Basketball Coach and Assistant Director of Athletics
1976–1981	Jefferson High School, Knoxville, Tennessee Secondary Physical Education Teacher and Head Girls' Basketball Coach; Chair, Girls' Physical Education Department, 1978–1981
1974–1976	Morgan State University, Baltimore, Maryland Teaching Assistant and Freshman Basketball Coach
1971–1972	Harriman YWCA, Harriman, Tennessee Assistant Program Director and Fitness Instructor

CAREER HIGHLIGHTS

1981	Selected Outstanding Coach, Michigan Region X Tournament
1980	Coached Tennessee State High School Championship AAA Girls' Basketball Team
1979	Appointed to Tennessee State Girls' Athletics Advisory Board
1975	Awarded Harriet McCown Scholarship for graduate study in Physical Education
1973	Elected Captain, Middle Tennessee State University Women's Basketball Team

PROFESSIONAL ACTIVITIES

1981	Representative, Faculty Council, Kellogg Community College
1980	Chair, Alumni Sports Foundation Fund, Middle Tennessee State University
1975	Member, Student Advisory Athletic Committee, Morgan State University
1980	Member, American Association of Health, Physical Education, and Recreation Member, American Association of University Women

EDUCATIONAL BACKGROUND

1974–1976	Morgan State University, Baltimore, Maryland M.A. - Physical Education
1972–1974	Middle Tennessee State University, Murfreesboro, Tennessee B.A. with distinction - Major: Physical Education; Minor: Psychology
1969–1971	Roane State Community College, Harriman, Tennessee A.A. - General Studies

PLACEMENT FILE

Center for Career Development, Coldspring Lane & Hillen Road
Morgan State University, Baltimore, Maryland 21230

SAMPLE VITA—COUNSELING

RHEA ANDREWS

1421 Bowery Street
Los Angeles, California 93210
(213) 244-3088—home
(213) 247-9247—office

EXPERIENCE SUMMARY

Associate Professor	five years
Counseling Center Director	three years
Assistant Professor	five years
Staff Counselor	two years

ACADEMIC BACKGROUND

Ph.D. REHABILITATION COUNSELING 1973
University of Miami, Miami, Florida

M.A. COUNSELING and HUMAN DEVELOPMENT 1969
Washington University, St. Louis, Missouri

B.A. CLASSICS 1966
Pepperdine University, Malibu, California

AREAS OF EXPERTISE

Rehabilitation Counseling and Research
Vocational Psychology
Behavioral Counseling and Psychotherapy
Clinical Assessment and Measurement
Rehabilitation and the Disabled

PROFESSIONAL OVERVIEW

Associate Professor, Counselor Education Department
University of California at Los Angeles (1978–present)

Responsible for teaching and program development in master's and doctoral degree programs in rehabilitation, community-based programs and counseling psychology.

Director of the UCLA Counseling Center (1980–present)

Responsible for budget design and maintenance, staffing, policies, and evaluation of the 12-member counseling staff.

Assistant Professor, Department of Educational Psychology
University of Florida, Gainesville, Florida (1973–1978)

Coordinated and supervised entry-level community-based practica. Responsibilities included teaching core courses in educational psychology, mental health services, and rehabilitation counseling.

Staff Counselor, Counseling Center
Lincoln University, Jefferson City, Missouri (1968–1970)

Coordinated career program development component. Responsibilities included counseling and psychological evaluations for the university community, primarily undergraduate students.

Dossier available from the Placement Center, Jessup Hall,
University of Miami, Miami, Florida 33103

SAMPLE VITA—COUNSELING

RHEA ANDREWS
Page 2

CURRENT PROFESSIONAL SERVICE

University of California at Los Angeles 1978—

Chair, Search Committee for University Counseling Center
Co-Chair, Graduate Admissions Council
Member, University Athletic Board
Member, Curriculum & Instructional Review Committee
Editorial Consultant, Higher Education Series, Jossey-Bass, Inc.,
    Publishers, San Francisco, California
Consultant, Rehabilitation Grants Program, U.S. Department of Education,
    Washington, D.C.

PUBLICATIONS

Handbook on Rehabilitation Programs for the Disabled, by Rhea Andrews,
Alan Publishing House, New York, 1980.

"The Realities of Rehabilitation Centers," by Rhea Andrews and Paul
Jasper, *Rehabilitation Counseling Bulletin,* 1979, Vol. 57.

"Interview Techniques for Rehabilitation Counselors," by Rhea Andrews,
Journal of Applied Rehabilitation Counseling, October, 1978, Vol. 63, No. 2.

"Inservice Training for Campus-based Counseling Centers," by Rhea Andrews
and Kevin Franker, *The Personnel and Guidance Journal,* January, 1981, Vol. 5.

MAJOR ADDRESSES

"The Role of the Supervisor in Counseling Centers," American Personnel and
Guidance Association National Convention, Chicago, April, 1982.

"Interview Behavior and Client Outcome," Western Association for Counselor
Education and Supervision Annual Conference, Salt Lake City, Utah,
October, 1981.

"Rehabilitation and the Role of the Family," Changing Family Conference IX,
The University of Iowa, Iowa City, Iowa, February, 1979.

AFFILIATIONS

National Rehabilitation Association
American Rehabilitation Counseling Association
American Education Research Association
American Personnel and Guidance Association
American Association of University Professors
Phi Delta Kappa

DISTINCTIONS

National Merit Scholar
Phi Beta Kappa
Magna Cum Laude
Executive Officer, Pepperdine Student Body
President, Washington University Graduate Student Senate

LICENSURE

Licensed psychologist in the states of Florida and California
Rehabilitation counselor, certified by National Commission on
    Rehabilitation Counseling
Certified consulting psychologist, Missouri State Board of Psychology

SAMPLE RÉSUMÉ—COUNSELOR EDUCATION

MICHAEL R. FRANKER

ADDRESSES:

Home	8 Monaco Parkway Rochester, New York 14603 (716) 988-5599	Office	21 Norman Hall University of Rochester Rochester, New York 14603 (716) 275-2385

EDUCATION:

University of Rochester Rochester, New York	1981–1983	MA	Counselor Education/ Student Personnel
Glassboro State College Glassboro, New Jersey	1979–1980		Counseling Psychology
Trenton State College Trenton, New Jersey	1975–1979	BS	Psychology/Computer Science with Distinction

RELATED PROFESSIONAL EXPERIENCE:

Graduate Assistantships

Academic Advisor, Undergraduate Advisory Office, University of Rochester, 1982–1983. Academic advising of underclass advisees and unassigned special non-degree students; interviewing students on academic probation, and responsible for organizing advance CLEP registration.

Teaching Assistant, Introductory Psychology, Glassboro State College, 1979–1980. Responsible for instruction and grade assignment for three 1-hour discussion sections per semester; included designing and grading quizzes, answering student questions and keeping office hours.

Practica

Career Development Office, University of Rochester, Fall, 1983. Assisted in the day-to-day operations of a comprehensive placement center. Advised seniors about résumé writing techniques and interview awareness. Reviewed current career literature in Resource Center.

Special Support Services, Spring Component, University of Rochester, Spring, 1982. Assisted staff with special projects; met with prospective minority and educationally disadvantaged students.

Orientation, University of Rochester, Summer, 1982. Assisted director with summer freshman orientation programs, and with special projects related to transfer students.

Group Leader, Human Relations Training Course, Glassboro State College, Spring, 1980. Conducted group communication exercises and led discussion groups once a week.

Counseling Center, Glassboro State College, Fall, 1980. Counseled under supervision, observed counselors in sessions and discussed cases.

SAMPLE RÉSUMÉ—COUNSELOR EDUCATION

MICHAEL R. FRANKER
Page 2

WORKSHOPS AND CONVENTIONS:

Program Co-Chair, "Micro Computers and Student Services," APGA/ACPA Convention, Detroit, Michigan, 1983.

Workshop Leader, "Advising the New Student," State Student Services Conference, Rochester, New York, 1982.

Discussion Facilitator, Regional Conference on Counseling, Pittsburgh, Pennsylvania, 1982.

Attended the ACPA Convention, Denver, Colorado, 1981.

PROFESSIONAL MEMBERSHIPS:

American College Personnel Association

American Personnel and Guidance Association

Graduate Student Development Association

SPECIAL INTERESTS:

Computer Programming (FORTRAN, COBOL, BASIC, RPGII)

Public Relations

Organizational Behavior

VOLUNTEER EXPERIENCE:

Part-time counselor and small-group leader, The First Avenue Half-Way House, Rochester, New York, 1982–present

Assistant, Free Medical Clinic, Rochester, New York, 1981–present

Patient Information Assistant, Trenton State Hospital, Trenton, New Jersey, 1977–1980

Big Brother, Pals Association, Trenton, New Jersey, 1975–1977

ACADEMIC HONORS:

Dean's List

Psi Chi, Undergraduate Honorary in Psychology

National Merit Scholarship Recipient

CREDENTIALS ON FILE:

Career Services and Placement Center, 224 Lattimore Hall, University of Rochester, Rochester, New York 14627   (716) 275-2366

SAMPLE RÉSUMÉ—SPEECH PATHOLOGY

KEVIN F. RAYE

130 Summit Street
Iowa City, Iowa 52240
(319) 351-9784

ACADEMIC BACKGROUND

The University of Iowa Iowa City, Iowa	M.A., 1983	Major—Speech Pathology
Grinnell College Grinnell, Iowa	B.S., 1981	Major—Biology

Will be qualified to provide speech and language services in hospitals, clinical settings and public schools, grades K–12.

PUBLIC SCHOOL EXPERIENCE

Speech Aide	Wilton Elementary School Wilton, Iowa	Fall	1982
Preschool Hearing & Language Screening	Wendell Johnson Clinic The University of Iowa	Spring	1983
Elementary Practicum	Penn Elementary School North Liberty, Iowa	Fall	1983

Worked primarily with language-impaired and learning-disabled children as well as with children with language disorders.

CLINICAL EXPERIENCE

Clinic:

Wendell Johnson Speech and Hearing Clinic	Articulation Disorders Voice Disorders	Spring Fall	1982 1982
The University of Iowa	Cleft Palate Aural Rehabilitation	Summer Fall	1983 1983

Hospitals:

St. Luke's Methodist Hospital Cedar Rapids, Iowa	Spring	1983

Involved remediation of adults with neuropathologies of speech and language and children with language disorders.

Department of Child Psychiatry Psychopathic Hospital Iowa City, Iowa	Spring	1983

Involved language remediation with emotionally disturbed children.

SAMPLE RÉSUMÉ—SPEECH PATHOLOGY

KEVIN F. RAYE
Page 2

TRAINING ASSIGNMENTS

Research Assistant	Otolaryngology Department University of Iowa Hospital	Fall	1982
Teaching Assistant	Clinical Procedures Course	Summer	1983

WORK EXPERIENCE

Lab Assistant	Biology Department Grinnell College	1979–1981
Counselor	Camp Sunnyside Des Moines, Iowa	Summers 1979 & 1980

COLLEGE DISTINCTIONS AND ACTIVITIES

Phi Kappa Phi
Phi Beta Kappa
Dean's List
Easter Seal Society Scholarship
National Science Foundation Undergraduate Research Grant
National Student Speech and Hearing Association

COMMUNITY SERVICE

United Way Fundraising Co-Chair	University Component Iowa City, Iowa	1982–1983
Citizens for Environmental Action, member	Eastern Iowa Chapter Iowa City, Iowa	1981–
Crisis Center Volunteer	Iowa City, Iowa	1981–1982

CREDENTIALS ON FILE

Educational Placement Office
N302 Lindquist Center
The University of Iowa
Iowa City, Iowa 52242
(319) 353-4365

SAMPLE RÉSUMÉ–SOCIAL WORK

LISA MARIE BAKER
21 Lincoln Place
Madison, Wisconsin 53711
(608) 271-4041–home
(608) 274-2012–office

———————————— PROFESSIONAL BACKGROUND ————————

FAMILY CASEWORKER, Bureau of Children's Services, Madison, Wisconsin, 1982–present. Responsible for coordinating home visits of all clients in central Wisconsin; arranging for medical services and follow-up on financial assistance. Promoted in 1983.

———————————— CAREER OBJECTIVE ————————————

Desire entry-level administrative position in a state social service agency.

———————— SOCIAL WORK FIELD EXPERIENCES ————————

MEDICAL SOCIAL WORKER, University of Wisconsin Hospitals, Madison, Wisconsin, Fall semester, 1981.

COMMUNITY LIAISON, Goodwill Industries of Central Wisconsin, Spring semester, 1981.

CASEWORKER, Lutheran Social Services, Madison, Wisconsin, Summer session, 1980.

Additional three-week hospital internships were completed in pediatric, psychiatric, and terminally ill units.

————————— GRADUATE COURSE CONCENTRATIONS ————————

Human Services Administration
Community Organizations
Advanced Concepts of Community and Family Health Nursing
Family Dynamics
Leadership in Groups
Social Change, Social Development, and Social Work

——————————————— EDUCATION ———————————————

Master of Social Work	University of Wisconsin–Madison Madison, Wisconsin	1980–1982
Bachelor of Science–Nursing	University of Wisconsin–LaCrosse LaCrosse, Wisconsin	1976–1980

——————————— PROFESSIONAL ASSOCIATIONS ————————

Academy of Certified Social Workers
National Association of Social Workers
American Public Health Association
Wisconsin Public Health Association

————————————— PRESENTATIONS ————————————

"Social Workers as Children's Advocates," major address at the Great Lakes Association of Social Workers, Gary, Indiana, October, 1983.

"Medical Professionals and Social Workers–How to Improve the Profession," Co-Chair, Midwest Conference on Health Services, Macomb, Illinois, Summer, 1982.

"Organizing Community Volunteers," Workshop leader, Conference on Volunteers, Wisconsin United Way Association, Madison, Wisconsin, Spring, 1980.

———————— REFERENCES FURNISHED UPON REQUEST ————————

Chapter Three

Building Effective Letters

Letter writing is a fundamental, universal, and critical step in any job search; it is also perceived by many job seekers as difficult, dull, and dismaying. Popular excuses or reasons to procrastinate include such things as lack of time, higher priorities, poor typing skills, an inferior typewriter (or none at all), limited knowledge of proper format and, finally, not knowing what or how much to say or how to say it. Most of us find it easier to communicate in person or by telephone and are not willing to take the time to organize our thoughts on paper, but perhaps the most paralyzing impediment to effective letter writing is the difficulty we have when we attempt to write about ourselves.

This chapter will not necessarily make letter writing easy but it will discuss and demonstrate elements of effective letters, beginning with the basic core and progressing to a complete, individualized, targeted letter. Just as a vita is constructed step by step and item by item, so are letters built from carefully calculated and discriminatingly selected bits and pieces. There are other similarities between developing a vita and a letter. Both are controlled by the writer so that the content emphasizes positive characteristics and attributes and minimizes, glosses over, or ignores weaknesses or gaps while slanting the material toward a specific objective. The letter is governed by the same cardinal rules as the vita— it must be visually pleasing, accurate and current, and error-free. The letter and the vita have identical goals—to draw attention to the writer as a viable candidate and to encourage the potential employer to arrange an interview to discuss the available position.

The major difference between a letter and a vita is that the letter can function independently. Vitas must always be accompanied by a cover letter (if they are not presented in person) but some of the letters used in the employment process may require no additions or enclosures. Unlike the vita, which is usually photocopied by one method or another, letters must be originals. Each one needs to be typed individually. The importance of original letters can be easily understood if you put yourself in the employer's place. One way to do this is to imagine that it is the holiday season. The annual exchange of holiday greetings and messages usually brings us more mail per day than at any other time of the year. Most of us begin by opening all of the envelopes to see who sent them and to see if notes are enclosed. Our attention is first drawn to messages that are concise and personalized. Later, as time permits, the purple ditto messages are scanned. The scenario is quite the same for employers and search committees. They are attracted to concise, personalized, individualized communications.

TYPES OF LETTERS

Most people think only of writing letters of application, but many other letters will be required in the employment process. Job seekers at any level will write some or all of the following letters during the job search:

- letter of inquiry
- letter of application
- letter of transmittal
- letter following the interview
- letter of contract acknowledgment
- letter of acceptance
- letter of refusal

Each letter should be approached with an awareness of its unique function and importance. Length and style will vary with each letter and each situation. The capsule descriptions below will clarify the objective and purpose of each of these seven letters.

LETTER OF INQUIRY

A letter of inquiry is sent to prospective employers to inquire if a vacancy exists or is anticipated. A copy of the vita should always be enclosed, but it is not necessary to submit supporting documents or supplementary materials. Most people, especially those who must limit their job search to a particular region or community, should not rely solely on advertised vacancies but take some initiative in contacting potential employers. Years ago, when the demand for new academics and professionals far exceeded the supply, it was not uncommon for job seekers to send out letters of inquiry to various parts of the country and to receive, in return, letters expressing interest in their qualifications and even occasional job offers. Today's job seekers should not anticipate that all letters of inquiry will receive a response; if vacancies do not exist, some departments or personnel offices may, as a standard practice, simply send a form letter acknowledging the inquiry or send no response at all. Nonetheless, even though it is a gamble against high odds, the inquiry system should not be ignored. It is not productive to blanket the country with letters of inquiry. Perhaps the best way to limit your search is to concentrate on job possibilities in a single geographic area. If for no other reason, letters of inquiry should be sent in order to make you feel that you have done all you can do to promote your own interests. However many letters you send and however few replies you receive, bear in mind that it takes only one positive response to produce the job you need.

LETTER OF APPLICATION

When you have learned of a vacancy for which you wish to be considered, send a letter of application. State clearly the position for which you are applying. It is customary to indicate how you learned of the vacancy. The body of the letter should be used to emphasize those aspects of your background and experience which relate most closely to the announced vacancy. A vita always accompanies this letter; the letter should refer the reader to this enclosure. If other supporting documents (transcripts, dossier, etc.) have been requested, state that they are enclosed or that they will be forwarded. The application letter should also indicate that you are willing to arrange an interview and to provide further information upon request.

LETTER OF TRANSMITTAL

After the initial contact has been made with an employer, you may be asked to provide samples of your work (writing samples, performance tapes, slides of artwork, coaching films, etc.). A letter of transmittal states that the requested materials are enclosed or are being sent under separate cover. This letter should be brief and to the point. Give relevant facts, but let the enclosures speak for themselves; do not provide a lengthy synopsis or detailed explanation of the contents. For the employer's convenience and for some assurance that the supporting materials will be returned, always enclose a stamped, self-addressed envelope.

LETTER FOLLOWING THE INTERVIEW

After returning from an interview (whether at a conference or at the institution or facility where the vacancy exists), a letter expressing appreciation for the interview is obligatory. In addition to being a professional courtesy, a follow-up letter can reemphasize important components of the interview or introduce a personal or academic strength which was omitted or inadequately covered during the interview. It is always appropriate to express continued interest in the position or, if you have decided that you would not accept an offer, the employer should be informed of your decision. If you are to be reimbursed for interview expenses, you may return the institution's expense voucher or a summary of your expenses. It is necessary to send a letter only to the principal interviewer, but it is often a good idea to mention the names of other persons involved in the selection process as well. Keep the tone of the letter positive and professional—your paths may cross again.

LETTER OF CONTRACT ACKNOWLEDGMENT

When you receive an offer but are not able to make an immediate decision to accept or decline, a letter acknowledging the receipt of the offer or contract should be sent promptly. The employer typically requests your decision within a certain time period. If you anticipate that you will not be able to reach a decision within the specified time, you may use this letter to request a reasonable extension. A delay of this type is not routine and should only be used in exceptional circumstances. Most often a decision to accept or reject a contract can be reached without resorting to this type of communication.

LETTER OF ACCEPTANCE

If you have decided to accept an offer received in person, by telephone, or by letter, your acceptance should be stated in writing. If a formal contract is offered, it should be signed and returned with a brief cover letter. If there is no formal contract, the letter of acceptance should clearly state the terms of the appointment including title of position, salary, and starting date. If the appointment is for a fixed term, the duration should be stated.

LETTER OF REFUSAL

If you have decided to decline an offer, a letter indicating your decision must be sent promptly. A verbal refusal should be confirmed in writing. It is always a good idea to express appreciation for the offer. It is not inappropriate to indicate reasons for refusing the offer if you wish to do so, but you are not obligated to explain your decision. As a professional, you want your letter to reflect tact and courtesy. Remember, it is a small world and future employment possibilities could be affected.

CORE SENTENCES FOR COVER LETTERS

Even before you find any jobs for which you can apply, you can begin constructing your cover letters by writing sentences describing your qualifications and experiences. Cover letters allow you to elaborate on particular experiences and strengths; don't depend upon your vita to tell the whole story. To begin the process, you might want to select items from your vita to be expanded in order to illustrate and amplify their importance. These sentences will form the core of a cover letter. You may be able to use the same sentences for many different letters, or you can modify them to suit a specific application. Select those sentences which are most applicable to the position for which you are applying. Preparing a series of core sentences in advance can make writing cover letters easier and faster. There is no need to stare at a blank page wondering what you are going to say, and application deadlines may not allow the time to write several drafts.

Developing core sentences for four major areas will simplify and expedite the task of writing cover letters. The following examples of core sentences based on the vita prepared by Christopher Asche (page 32) illustrate how information from the vita could be presented in the text of a cover letter.

- Academic Training

  As a Robert Fay Literary Fellow in 1981-82 at Cambridge University, I began the research for my dissertation which is currently in progress and will be completed next year.

- Selected Research

  My dissertation, "Aesthetic Distance in the Early Comedies of Ben Jonson," focuses on Jonson's use of comic distortion and fable to achieve aesthetic distance.

- Teaching Experience

  As a teaching assistant in the Communications Program at Arizona State University, I was responsible for all aspects of a required freshman course, including instruction and grading as well as individual conferences and student advising.

- Activities and Achievements

  While a student member of the Southwest Modern Language Association I presented a paper based on a chapter of my dissertation, "Myth and Fabliau: Sources for Jonson's Volpone," *at the annual conference in Phoenix, Arizona.*

TARGETING YOUR LETTER FROM THE TOP DOWN

In order to target a letter toward a specific position or institution, it is always necessary to include information that will individualize and personalize your letter. Targeted letters do some or all of the following:

- address an individual by name and appropriate title

- indicate the exact title of the announced position (and position number if applicable)
- state how you learned of the position
- mention the institution by official name
- refer to relevant information about the department or institution
- relate qualifications to job description
- specify application procedures which are being followed (dossier, transcripts, portfolio, interview arrangements, etc.)

SALUTATION

Developing a targeted letter begins with the inside address and the salutation. Whenever possible, address the letter to a specific person, using full name and exact title. Don't underestimate the importance of the salutation in your eagerness to begin the body of the letter. The salutation offers more opportunity for error than any other part of your letter. Frequently used but not recommended salutations from the following list amuse some professionals, offend others, and impress none.

If gender or a title is in question, it is acceptable to address the reader as Dear Professor Blank rather than risk offending with an incorrect title (Mr., Miss, Ms., Mrs.). In a case where no name is indicated on the job announcement, a preferred and perfectly acceptable alternative is to omit the salutation completely. This is less awkward than using an informal, trite, stock phrase. If the salutation is omitted, you should also omit the complimentary closing. (See letter of application on page 54.)

BLACKLIST OF DEAD-END SALUTATIONS

Dear Head	Dear Ma'am	Sirs
Dear Chair	Dear Ladies	Ladies
Dear Chairman	Dear Search Committee	Mesdames
Dear Dean	Dear Faculty Member	Friends and Colleagues
Dear Person	Dear Director	To Whom It May Concern
Dear People	Dear Colleague	Good Morning
Dear Gentlepeople	Dear Friends	
Dear Sir	Gentlemen	

INTRODUCTION

Avoid ambiguity. In order for your letter to receive proper handling and attention, the first paragraph must state clearly the exact title of the position for which you wish to be considered a candidate. It is also a good idea to let the reader know how you learned of the opening.

BODY

The body of the letter consists of one or more paragraphs highlighting your qualifications. Concentrate on experiences related to the duties and responsibilities presented in the position announcement. Refer to your enclosed vita and expand upon relevant items. Some advertised positions list several areas of responsibility or expertise. Candidates matching several, but perhaps not all, of the stated areas can and should apply. The position may be adjusted to suit the person considered best qualified. Emphasize the positive and ignore the weak areas. Do not apologize for not meeting the exact qualifications requested.

CONCLUSION

The concluding paragraph will vary depending upon the items contained in the introduction and body of your letter. The main thrust of a concluding paragraph should be your interest in discussing the position and your qualifications more fully in an interview. Stating that supporting documents (dossier, transcripts, portfolio, etc.) are available, enclosed, or being forwarded is also appropriate as part of the conclusion.

DRAFT, REVISE—AND KEEP COPIES

Don't expect to write a perfect letter the first time around. The immediate goal should be a draft which presents the material in an organized, coherent fashion and in a style suited both to you and to your reader. This type of communication calls for a professional, straightforward tone. False modesty and humility are not virtues, but neither are pomposity and boastfulness. Don't underestimate the importance of sharing your accomplishments with the reader, but let the reader be impressed by your achievements rather than your narration.

There may be someone, somewhere, who is capable of writing a humorous letter of application successfully—but most such attempts fail and fail badly. A sense of humor is a wonderful gift but you will have opportunities to display your wit and cleverness at a later stage of the selection process. Be cautious of any variation from standard, formal communication in either style or format. Anything other than a fairly straightforward letter tends to smack of desperation.

The length and appearance of the letter, as well as its content, will have an impact on the reader. Employers generally prefer brief and concise communications and this should always be your goal. If you can convey all of the information relevant to the position in one page it is to your advantage to do so. Because some positions are multifaceted, however, it may be necessary to use more than one page to present your qualifications. Let common sense, rather than arbitrary rules, be your guide for the length of your letter. For ease in reading, use a good typewriter with a clear, black ribbon. Select stationery of good quality matching or coordinating with the paper used for the vita.

Keep a copy of all correspondence with prospective employers in your personal file for documentation and future reference. These copies will help you keep track of what you have sent to whom, when, and where. If you are invited to an interview, the copies will enable you to review all correspondence with that employer. Maintaining complete and accurate records of your job search is an essential part of the total employment process and should not be viewed as an inconvenience or a bother.

MAINTAINING CONTACTS

You cannot assume that your work is finished once the initial contact has been made. In order to keep your inquiry or application from disappearing into the employer's files, contacts must be maintained through follow-up letters or even personal visits. While it is always proper to make the initial contact by letter, a subsequent contact can also be made by telephone or in person. Arranging an appointment to meet the administrator or department head is preferable, but even dropping by unannounced can allow you to introduce yourself and let the employer know that you are currently available and that you remain interested in possible openings. Use good judgment in the frequency of your contacts; you want to be sure that employers are aware of your continued interest but you do not want to be labeled a pest. Occasional follow-ups by mail, telephone, or personal visit assure that you will maintain professional contact and allow you to be aware of any developments which could affect your chances for employment.

SAMPLE LETTERS

Examples of the main types of letters you will most likely have to write are presented on the following pages. They are: letter of inquiry, letter of application, letter of transmittal, letter following the interview, letter of contract acknowledgment, letter of acceptance, and letter of refusal.

SAMPLE LETTER OF INQUIRY

121 Communications Center
Arizona State University
Tempe, Arizona 85281
February 21, 1983

Joseph Hayen, Chairman
Department of English
Reed College
2121 Woodstock Boulevard
Portland, Oregon 97202

Dear Professor Hayen:

I am writing to inquire if you anticipate a vacancy in the English department at Reed College for which I might be considered. My course work for the Ph.D. has been completed at Arizona State University and I am currently working on my dissertation.

As you will note from the enclosed vita, my teaching experience has concentrated on the development of speaking and writing skills. As a teaching assistant in the Communications Program at Arizona State University, I was responsible for all aspects of a required freshman course, including instruction and grading as well as individual conferences and student advising. Last year I was selected to serve as a research assistant with Professors Gould and Perry in the implementation of a federally funded grant to introduce a new undergraduate program in expository writing.

I am genuinely interested in the teaching of writing and I chose to include expository writing as one area of my comprehensive exams. My master's program at The Ohio State University and my doctoral studies have given me a broad background in literature. I am qualified and interested in teaching survey courses in both British and American literature and upper-division courses in British literature from the Renaissance through the Victorian era.

As a graduate of Hiram College, I have a particular interest in working with undergraduates at a small liberal arts college. If you anticipate a vacancy, please use the enclosed self-addressed stamped envelope to inform me of application procedures. My dossier and supporting documents will be sent upon request.

Sincerely yours,

Christopher J. Asche

Christopher J. Asche

Enc.

SAMPLE LETTER OF APPLICATION

421 Walnut
Tempe, Arizona 85281
April 10, 1983

Search Committee
Department of English
310 Wesbrook Hall
University of Denver
University Park
Denver, Colorado 80210

I would like to be considered as an applicant for the position of instructor in the University of Denver English department which was announced in the February Job List of the Modern Language Association. I am a candidate for a Ph.D. in English at Arizona State University. My dissertation, "Aesthetic Distance in the Early Comedies of Ben Jonson," focuses on Jonson's use of comic distortion and fable to achieve aesthetic distance. Research for the dissertation was begun with Professor Walter Wesley during my year at Cambridge University as a Robert Fay Literary Fellow. My dissertation advisor at Arizona State University is Professor Dale Maurice.

I am genuinely interested in the teaching of writing and I chose to include expository writing as one area of my comprehensive exams. As the enclosed vita indicates, I have had experience in both teaching and research in this area. As a teaching assistant in the Communications Program at Arizona State University, I was responsible for all aspects of a required freshman course, including instruction and grading as well as individual conferences and student advising. During the current year I have been responsible for compiling an annotated bibliography and review of the literature pertaining to methods of teaching expository writing as a part of a federal grant administered by Professors Gould and Perry.

My complete dossier is being sent to you from the Placement Center at Arizona State University. If there are additional application materials to be completed, please contact me. I would welcome the opportunity to discuss this position with you in person and can be available for an interview at your convenience.

Christopher J. Asche

Christopher J. Asche

Enc.

SAMPLE LETTER OF TRANSMITTAL

1205 E. College
Des Moines, Iowa 50316
February 7, 1983

John Gere
Director, Evening School
The Cleveland Institute of Art
1141 East Boulevard
University Circle
Cleveland, Ohio 44106

Dear Mr. Gere:

As you requested in your letter of February 2, I am enclosing twenty slides of my recent ceramics work. Additional slides of my work and of my students' work are available and can be furnished if desired. A self-addressed, stamped, return envelope is enclosed for your convenience.

I would be very interested in discussing in more detail the opening for a ceramics instructor in your evening program. If any additional information is required, please let me know.

Sincerely yours,

Brendan McConnell

Brendan McConnell

Encs.

SAMPLE LETTER FOLLOWING THE INTERVIEW

6200 28th Avenue North
Minneapolis, Minnesota 55427
October 1, 1983

Beverly Maye, Director
Laramie Public Library
2 Mountain View Lane
Laramie, Wyoming 82071

Dear Ms. Maye:

The opportunity to visit with you and to become acquainted with the facilities of your library has strengthened my interest in the reference librarian position now available. I was particularly interested in the plans to convert to a computerized card catalog and I feel that my background would enable me to make a strong contribution to this effort.

Thank you for the time and consideration shown to me during my visit. I especially appreciated the tour of Laramie with your assistant, Paula Ray. As you mentioned at the conclusion of our interview, I will anticipate hearing from you regarding your decision after October 12.

Sincerely,

Janine Swenson

Janine Swenson

SAMPLE LETTER OF CONTRACT ACKNOWLEDGMENT

21 Lincoln Place
Madison, Wisconsin 53711
June 15, 1983

Iris Wilken
Adult Program Coordinator
Division of Community Services
Department of Social Services
Lansing, Michigan 48829

Dear Ms. Wilken:

I wish to express my appreciation for the offer of the Program Coordinator II position in your division. As we discussed in our telephone conversation, I am considering a similar position with the Division of Children and Family Services in Springfield, Illinois.

I will contact you as soon as I have made a decision, but no later than June 28. Each position has features that I find challenging and appealing and I will give careful consideration to your offer.

Sincerely,

Lisa Marie Baker

Lisa Marie Baker

SAMPLE LETTER OF ACCEPTANCE

429 Oak Street, #421B
Lafayette, Indiana 47906
April 3, 1983

Dr. Doug Robertson
Head, Department of Chemistry
N201 Chemistry Building
University of South Carolina
Columbia, South Carolina 29208

Dear Dr. Robertson:

I am pleased to accept your offer of an appointment as an assistant professor in your department at an annual salary of $25,000. As you know, I will be teaching a course during the summer term at Purdue and will be available to begin my duties at the University of South Carolina on August 26, 1983.

During my visit to your campus, I was very impressed with your facilities and the faculty in your department. The opportunity to work with undergraduates and to conduct the graduate Seminar in Organic Chemistry is especially appealing. I look forward to joining you and your staff.

Sincerely,

Denise Overman

Denise Overman

SAMPLE LETTER OF REFUSAL

1421 Bowery Street
Los Angeles, California 93210
June 24, 1983

Dr. J. Donovan Lind
President
Boston University
Administration Boulevard
Boston, Massachusetts 02215

Dear President Lind:

After careful thought and deliberation, I have decided to continue in my present position at the University of California at Los Angeles. This was a difficult decision and I sincerely appreciate the offer of the position of Associate Vice President for Student Services.

My husband and I would like to thank you for the courtesy extended during our visit. I was impressed with the quality of the services provided at Boston University and the professional attitude of your faculty and staff. I am sure that the person selected will enjoy working with your fine university community.

Sincerely yours,

Rhea Andrews

Rhea Andrews

Chapter Four

Interviewing, Considering Offers, and Making Decisions

Critical as each stage of the selection process may be, most job seekers express particular anxiety about and interest in the interview. There is some justification for placing so much importance on the personal interview. All of the preceding stages aim toward this encounter. No vita, cover letter, or dossier—however glowing—will get you a job; their purpose is to stimulate an employer's interest in your qualifications so that a face-to-face meeting will be arranged.

There is no shortage of advice about interviewing. Everyone who has ever participated in an interview situation—on either side of the desk—has an opinion to offer and a collection of anecdotes ranging from horror stories to brilliant successes. Whether you are a first-time job seeker or an experienced professional, you probably do not consider yourself an expert on the subject of interviewing. It is important to recognize that some of the people responsible for hiring do not have a great deal of experience in conducting interviews either. In many cases, especially in the academic world, they are teachers, researchers, practitioners, or administrators—not personnel specialists. Because they are not necessarily skilled interviewers, you must be prepared to guide the conversation if necessary so that your qualifications are presented and your questions answered. On the other hand, if you are applying for a position with a large corporation or research institute, or for a job with the federal government, it is quite likely that your initial interview will be conducted by a recruitment specialist who has the ability to present information and elicit responses so skillfully that the interview resembles a pleasant, flowing, professional conversation. In either event, the more you know about the processes and techniques of interviewing, the better you are able to control the exchange of information and the direction of the interview.

A good interview doesn't just happen. In order to make the situation work for you, it is essential that you devote some time to planning and preparing for each of the elements involved in the interview process. Because every interview will be different, you will need to prepare for each one individually; however, in spite of the differences, all interviews share some common features. Perhaps the most obvious similarity for the job seeker is the fact that all interviews tend to produce stress. Because you can never know exactly how the interview will proceed, what questions will be asked, or how you will be received, some anxiety is inevitable. The tension is heightened by the fact that you know you are competing with other well-qualified candidates for the position. You also recognize that, regardless of the outcome, personal and professional risks are involved. There is always the risk that you will not be selected for the position. Rejection almost always produces a blow to the ego since most job seekers interpret rejection as a failure even though the hiring official may attempt to assure them that they were excellent candidates with superior qualifications. In addition to personal disappointment, not getting the job is a professional setback because the job search must continue through another round of applications and interviews. It is also stressful to realize that if you are offered the job you will be forced to make decisions that will have both immediate and long-range implications for the development of your career and your personal life.

No amount of advance preparation can alleviate all of the anxieties attendant upon interviewing, but thorough planning can help you reduce the tensions and allow you to focus on the important elements of presenting yourself as a professional. This chapter can help you to make the most of any interview situation by calculating your strategies for:

- gathering information
- knowing what to expect
- organizing materials
- making a good first impression
- anticipating questions
- evaluating interview performance
- following through
- considering offers and making decisions

GATHERING INFORMATION

A basic step toward successful interviewing is learning as much as you can about the institution or organization and the specific department in which the vacancy exists. Gathering information can benefit you in several ways as you prepare for the interview. It will help you anticipate questions you may be asked and questions you will want to raise, provide material for conversation at informal receptions or other functions, and will certainly give you greater confidence in projecting the professional image that will maximize your chances for success during the interview.

Academics seeking faculty, research, or administrative positions can find basic facts about postsecondary institutions in Peterson's Annual Guides to Graduate Study/Book 1, published annually, which gives profiles of all institutions, including all graduate degrees offered in each graduate school and college, financial aid, accreditation, student services, library and computer facilities, and names of administrators and deans. In addition, other volumes in the Guides series offer specific details about graduate departments and programs, including faculty members' individual research projects, application-acceptance ratio, number of openings, makeup of the student body, the campus social climate, and community features. For job-hunting purposes you can learn a great deal by looking at the specific information offered for faculty members, such as the date of undergraduate and graduate degrees and institutions attended. This information can tell you the approximate age of the faculty and the ratio of men and women at various ranks.

College catalogs also can be useful sources of information. Your local academic library may have a collection of individual catalogs or a file of catalogs on microfiche. If a current catalog is not available locally, you may request one from the admissions office of any institution.

The directories prepared by many professional associations can give you additional information about departments. The *Guide to Graduate Departments of Sociology*, for example, published by the American Sociological Association, identifies areas of specialization for each department and lists dissertation titles and current employment status of recent graduates.

If you are seeking a position closely related to your academic preparation but outside the academic world, you will find a number of special directories for many different types of organizations, including hospitals, libraries, museums, and specific industries such as information services, recreation, or publishing. Many directories provide information not only about the organization or firm but also about executives, department heads, and other key personnel.

Once you have identified faculty members or other personnel in the department you hope to join, you can do a quick search to determine if any of them have published articles or books. Reading their published materials will give you insight into their research interests and areas of expertise and perhaps into their philosophies, attitudes, and inclinations. If you do not find any items published by current members of the department, do not rush to the conclusion that research and productivity are not priority items. Exercise caution in interpreting available data; the search committee may be looking for an individual who has a strong publication record or has at least the potential to generate substantial publications. Similarly, the fact that a department may have no women of senior rank or in executive positions should not lead you to conclude that women cannot be promoted, nor should you assume that you could not be hired simply because there are no current professional staff or faculty members from your university or comparable institutions.

The amount of time required to gather information about institutions and departments may seem burdensome, but the efforts can be productive and rewarding. No one has ever been too knowledgeable for an interview, but many job seekers have found reasons to regret their inadequate preparation.

KNOWING WHAT TO EXPECT

In addition to gathering information about the organization or institution, it will be helpful for you to know as much as you can about the purpose and the procedures for each interview. The selection process for academics and other professionals often involves two distinct types of interviews. Screening interviews, designed to identify candidates whose qualifications merit serious consideration, are typically conducted by recruiters visiting college campuses or attending professional conferences. Selection interviews, usually conducted at the employer's location, are designed to identify the individual whose qualifications, background, and personal characteristics are best suited to the available position. Understanding the nature and objective of these two types of interviews will help you to prepare for each situation.

SCREENING INTERVIEWS

Whether conducted at conferences or on college campuses, screening interviews are usually brief, perhaps a half hour in length. Both the interviewer and the applicant should be prepared to channel their energies toward an exchange of information which will most efficiently use the allotted time. In-depth interviewing is not the goal; minor details will probably not be discussed and there may not be time for comments or questions about the community or geographic area. There will be time to gather this information later. Screening interviews, to be productive, must be limited in scope but it should be possible for the applicant to gain a clear understanding of the duties and responsibilities of the available position and for the interviewer to gather the necessary information to assess the applicant's qualifications.

Interviews at conferences are a common practice in many professions because the opportunity to schedule a considerable number of interviews in one location is economically advantageous to the employer as well as to the applicant. It is obviously preferable to prearrange conference interviews, although it is often possible to meet with potential employers without a scheduled interview. Recruiters or hiring officials at conferences may choose to interview all interested applicants or they may allow interviews by invitation only.

If you are a graduate student, you should be sure faculty members from your department know that you are attending the conference and that you are available for interviews. Let them know how to reach you during the conference. Their contacts with colleagues from other institutions can be extremely helpful in arranging interviews for you. It is a good idea to give one or more copies of your vita to any faculty member who is familiar with your work and with your objective (especially those who have written references for you) and, of course, you will want to take extra copies of your vita to distribute to potential employers. Your primary purpose in attending the conference may be to interview for as many jobs as possible, but you should also plan to attend meetings and sessions related to your interests and areas of specialization. There is always the chance that participation in informal discussions can lead to a job prospect. Be visible, be assertive, and be professional, and don't hesitate to let people know you are looking for a job.

SELECTION INTERVIEWS

After the pool of applicants for a given position has been screened—through either preliminary interviews or evaluation of each candidate's letter of application, vita, and dossier—the finalists will be invited for a comprehensive, detailed interview or series of interviews. If you are invited for an "on-site" interview at the employer's location, you can expect that the field has been narrowed to a select group of candidates, although the exact number of finalists will vary with the nature of the organization and the level of the position. The amount of time devoted to a selection interview will also vary, but it is unlikely that an in-depth interview will be accomplished in less than an hour. For academic positions, it is not uncommon for an interview to extend to a full day or even longer.

During the course of a selection interview you can expect to meet with several different individuals involved in the selection process. It is possible for interviewing and hiring to be the responsibility of only one person, such as the director of a unit or a department head, but it is more common for the responsibility to be shared with a number of people who constitute a search committee. Search committees may be composed of unit directors or supervisors, staff members, and representatives of the community. In academic settings, search committees can be made up of administrators, faculty members from one or more departments, and students (graduate or undergraduate). Other members of the committee could include staff, Affirmative Action officials, or other interested parties who serve in a nonvoting or ex-officio capacity. Search committees for entry-level faculty or staff positions may consist of members of a single department or unit; committees formed for the purpose of selecting an administrator are more likely to consist of all of the individuals mentioned above.

Regardless of the size or makeup of the search committee, all committees will have a designated head, under whose direction responsibilities are divided among the voting members (generally an odd number). Typical responsibilities of a search committee include:

- disseminating the job description
- receiving and reviewing applications
- selecting individuals to be interviewed
- offering interview invitations
- scheduling interviews
- conducting interviews
- post-interview evaluation
- ranking of candidates
- Affirmative Action review
- recommending selected finalists to hiring official

In most cases, search committees do not have the power to hire. It is their function to recommend one or more candidates to the administrator ultimately responsible for hiring, subject to approval by the governing board of the institution or organization.

When you accept an invitation to interview, it is important to be aware of the interview schedule or timetable. The invitation may be accompanied by a detailed schedule of events, but if the information is incomplete or sketchy, asking the following questions is not only appropriate but essential for interview success:

- Will I meet with individuals or with the search committee as a group?
- Will I be expected to make a presentation? teach a class? perform a recital?
- Will I be able to observe classes? see the work setting?
- Will I meet potential colleagues? students?
- Will there be special functions (receptions, luncheons, etc.)?

Your preparation, the materials that you bring along, the wardrobe you select, and the arrangements for transportation and hotel accommodations hinge on basic schedule information. If you are expected to remain overnight, some employers will make arrangements for accommodations. If you are not informed of such arrangements, do not assume they will be made. Take the responsibility to reserve a hotel room. You can always cancel your reservations upon arrival if you find that other arrangements have been made. It is not inappropriate to inquire about the availability and proximity of hotels during the conversation inviting you to interview, but if you initiate the inquiry you should plan to make the arrangements and to cover the expenses.

The issue of transportation is much like that of lodgings. If assistance is offered, take advantage of it; if not, be prepared to handle the arrangements on your own. Never make special requests to be picked up or delivered to your hotel or to the airport. Many employers will automatically volunteer to provide these services in order to make your visit as comfortable and pleasant as possible. Regardless of what may happen, you must be independent and prepared to act on your own initiative.

Social functions including receptions or meals may be arranged to allow the applicant to meet potential colleagues. It is important to realize that social functions are part of the selection process. Guests are evaluating your social adeptness, poise, and personality. Keep in mind that committee members are looking for approachable, congenial colleagues, though not necessarily for close personal friends.

Everything you do and say throughout the interview schedule will be evaluated for what it reveals about both your abilities and suitabilities. The people you come into contact with will be attempting to discover your attitudes about your field, your education, and your experiences as well as your reactions to their institution and community. Your comments and actions generally will have a cumulative effect; yet a seemingly harmless comment or gesture can do you irreparable harm. Rarely are you given two chances to make a good impression, so do everything you can to ensure that your first impression will be positive. Let your sense of humor show, but not at anyone's expense. You are evaluated by how you are perceived; be cautious, but be yourself.

A SPECIAL NOTE ABOUT EXPENSES

Always have enough cash on hand to cover both expected and unexpected expenses. Travel and lodging represent the major portion of interview expenses but meals, cabs, and other incidentals can add up to a considerable sum. Keep all of your receipts for tax purposes or to be returned with your travel vouchers if you are to be reimbursed. Some institutions will reimburse you for any related interviewing expenses; others specify exactly what will be covered. There may be restrictions on reimbursement. For example, if the job is offered and you accept the offer, all expenses may be paid. If you decline the offer, the institution may reimburse you for half of the cost, or none at all. Before you accept an invitation to interview, make sure you understand the financial arrangements. However, if the interview is close to your home, do not push the issue of expenses; always use tact and common sense.

ORGANIZING MATERIALS

Planning your interview strategy involves preparation of supporting materials which can be used to facilitate the exchange of information. You will find it helpful to organize an interview packet containing the following relevant materials:

- several copies of your vita
- transcripts
- references and evaluations
- selected items from application portfolio
- copies of all correspondence with interviewing institution

The packaging of this material is a matter of personal preference. A simple file folder may be sufficient or you may prefer to use a notebook or an attaché case. Regardless of how you organize these materials, they must be easily accessible and relatively inconspicuous. Presenting selected items from your interview packet at appropriate times can give the impression of a highly organized professional. Inappropriate use of the same materials can be distracting and a waste of valuable interview time. Recognize that these materials are supplemental and must be used judiciously if at all. Always be prepared to present the materials to illustrate a point or in response to a question but do not plan a presentation around them. Whether or not you use the materials, organizing a packet will assist you in reviewing for the interview and will bolster confidence in your ability to handle interview situations.

MAKING A GOOD FIRST IMPRESSION

It is obvious that gathering information and organizing relevant papers are important steps in successful interviewing. Another important step is planning your wardrobe. Most job seekers assume that they will be spending money on the job search; vita production, stationery, postage, and interview expenses are accepted as necessary budget items. When it comes to choosing interview attire, making do with what you have may be a false economy. Faculty and staff members and employers in other professions are aware of the financial strain on graduate students and young professionals but regardless of the employer's level of empathy, the job seeker who makes the best overall impression will be the one who is ultimately selected. Consciously or unconsciously, people do make judgments based on appearance, and you need to look as good in person as you did on paper.

A suit, or at least a sports coat and tie, should be considered standard interview attire for men. For daytime interviews a sports coat with coordinating slacks is acceptable. A suit is preferred for evening receptions or functions. Dresses and suits are standard interview outfits for women, and dresses are always preferred for evening wear. Use common sense in choosing interview attire; always select clothing you feel comfortable in, always dress to your physical advantage, and always select attire that is appropriate for the position.

Don't be misled by the habitual appearance of your instructors or academic colleagues. Because of the casual, more relaxed attitude about appearance that prevails on many campuses and the typical range of academic salaries, professors are rarely placed on anyone's best-dressed list. Those who do attempt to make a statement by the way they dress are likely to strive for an aura of nonconformity, shabby elegance, or genteel poverty. Depending upon your field and the level of the position for which you are applying, a good rule of thumb might be to dress for an interview a little more formally or conservatively than you would expect to dress for a typical workday on the job. For example, a studio artist and a professor of economics will dress very differently in their everyday work situations and may dress somewhat differently for interviews. An artist in a sports coat may be as appropriately dressed as an economist in a three-piece suit.

Regardless of your field or the level of the position for which you are applying, it is possible to calculate your appearance so that you do not run the risk of harming your professional image or offending a potential employer. For any interview, these items are out:

- loud colors or unusual patterns
- plunging necklines (for either sex)
- extreme hemlines (maxi or mini)
- jeans
- leisure suits
- suntops or muscle shirts
- chiffon dresses
- extreme hairdos
- excessive jewelry

- heavy perfume/after-shave
- sunglasses
- hunting boots, sneakers, sandals, or moccasins
- scuffed shoes

Finally, if your interview situation requires travel and a change of clothing, plan ahead. The best traveler is a light traveler. Choose clothing that will pack well and will fit into one bag. Your image will not be enhanced if you require assistance with excessive baggage.

Appropriate attire and immaculate grooming are vitally important in creating a first impression, but you also need to consider your physical well-being. The night before the interview should be devoted to rest and relaxation. The interview will produce enough stress and exhaustion without putting yourself through a long cramming session the night before. Plan to get adequate rest, eat sensibly, and drink only moderately, if at all. Your interview performance depends on your ability to be alert and articulate.

ANTICIPATING QUESTIONS

Many new job seekers expect the interview to resemble an oral examination. It is true that some hiring officials or members of an academic search committee tend to ask probing questions about recent work experiences or research, especially the dissertation. If you are invited to make a presentation, be prepared to field tough content and theoretical questions about your topic and your research methods. You should be aware, however, that long before the interview the committee has begun to form opinions about your achievements and potential through an examination of your vita, an analysis of the references in your dossier, your published work, writing samples you submitted, and even, perhaps, by direct contact with your mentor, principal teachers, or current or previous employer.

It is not unusual and you should not be surprised to find that the majority of the questions are oriented toward other aspects of your qualifications. These questions, which may seem simpler and less academic, can prove to be even more critical because they reveal more about your attitudes, character, and personality than do questions focusing only on specifics of your academic training or experience. You must be ready and willing to express your viewpoints on a number of wide-ranging topics. Questions will vary with the type of institution or organization. Church-related organizations, small private colleges, specialized schools, and large research-centered institutions have particular needs and concerns. If you have taken the time to become familiar with basic facts about the employing institution you should be able to anticipate relevant questions.

Applicants for academic and professional positions can expect to encounter many of the following questions:

- Why did you apply for this position?

- How does your training relate to this opening?

- Why did you decide to become an educator? (or researcher or librarian, etc.)

- Why did you choose to do your graduate work at X University?

- When do you expect your degree to be granted?

- How did you choose your dissertation topic?

- Think of the two or three teachers who have had the most influence on you and tell why.

- Who were your principal teachers?

- Have you had any experience with grant applications?

- Have you submitted articles for publication?

- How would you describe your style of teaching? counseling? administration?

- How do you feel this department contributes to the overall goals of this institution?

- What in your background will help you make special contributions?

- Would you be willing to perform on-site supervision of student internships?

- Would you be willing to be active in departmental or campus committees?

- How do you balance research and teaching?

- What are your current research interests?

- What do you find most satisfying about teaching?

- What courses could you teach in addition to those we have discussed?

- Are there courses you prefer to teach? not to teach?

- Would you be willing to teach a related course in another department?

- Would you be willing to team-teach a required course for lower-division students?

- Would you be interested in summer teaching?

- Would you consider teaching a survey course for non-majors?

- Would you be willing to sponsor a club for majors in this department?

- What courses outside your field would you encourage your students to take?
- Would it ever be possible for every student in one of your classes to earn an A?
- Would you encourage a good student to switch majors?
- How do you feel about a student wishing to obtain a double major?
- The college attempts to influence a student's character as well as academic development. Is this compatible with your philosophy of education?
- Because of this college's religious affiliation, we consider moral and spiritual values an integral part of the educational process. Would you be comfortable with this philosophy?
- Do you believe that a faculty member should only be concerned with a student's academic problems?
- Would you plan to attend extracurricular activities in which your students may be involved?

QUESTIONS YOU SHOULDN'T BE ASKED

Anyone preparing for an interview should be aware that federal and state guidelines have been established regarding the type of information which can be requested. Questions regarding race, religion, or national origin are always inappropriate; other questions may be considered potentially discriminatory and are inappropriate or illegal unless they are asked of each applicant. Because the interviewers you will encounter are seldom personnel specialists, it is quite possible that some inappropriate questions may be raised innocently with no intent to discriminate. Whatever the questioner's intention may be, you are not obligated to answer the following questions:

- Do you wish to be addressed as Miss or Mrs.?
- Do you mind answering some personal questions?
- Do you plan on living in this community?
- How long do you expect to work for us?
- What is your spouse's occupation?
- Whom should we notify in case of an emergency?
- Where do your parents live and what do they do for a living?
- When and where were you born?

- When did you become a citizen of the U.S.?
- What is your native language?
- How did you learn to read/write/speak a foreign language?
- What is your religious affiliation?
- Of what societies/clubs/lodges are you a member?
- What is your military experience?
- Have you ever been arrested?
- Would you please submit a photograph with your application materials?
- What is your marital status?
- What type of military discharge did you receive?
- What was your maiden name?
- Are you now pregnant?
- Do you have children?
- Who cares for your children while you are at work?
- Are you the principal wage earner of your household?
- Do you have a disability?
- Have you ever had a drug-related problem?
- Do you use drugs or alcohol?
- Have you ever been treated for a mental or emotional problem?

If you are asked any questions of this type, you should realize that you have more than one option. If you feel that your answer will not be to your disadvantage, you can simply provide the information requested. You can also answer the question but let the interviewer know that this type of question is inappropriate. For example, in response to a question about your marital status, you could respond, "Yes, I've been married for several years, but I don't consider that fact pertinent to my career plans." You might also respond with a question, such as, "Do you see my marital status as significant to my qualifications for this position?" For some questions, especially those that relate to emergency contacts or number of dependents (which can be required for insurance coverages or other employee benefits), you may indicate that the information will be provided upon employment. Another response to an inappropriate question might be to sidestep the question but offer information that will concentrate on your skills and abilities. If you are asked about child-care arrangements, for example, you might answer, "I am as well organized in my personal life as I am in my professional responsibilities, and I am confident that this will not pose a problem." You should clearly

72

understand that you are not obligated to answer inappropriate or discriminatory questions and, if you choose not to provide the information, you should decline politely but firmly. Whether you see these questions as unnerving, frustrating, or even amusing, if you have prepared for the possibility of encountering inappropriate or discriminatory questions you will be able to respond without intimidation, guilt, or discomfiting embarrassment.

HOW YOU SAY IT IS IMPORTANT, TOO

Your response to any question will be judged not only on the content but on the manner in which you reply. The tone and quality of your voice and your manner of speaking play a significant role in the image you project. Nonverbal cues or body language are also important elements. Excessive gesturing, exaggerated facial expressions, fidgeting, slouching, or any nervous mannerisms are distracting and detract from the information you are offering and the impression you want to create. By listening carefully and thinking before you respond you should be able to control what you say and how you say it.

ALWAYS

- evaluate the question
- be ready to give examples
- be thorough but concise
- enunciate clearly and be audible
- be positive

NEVER

- mislead, lie, or deceive
- give vague, general, ambiguous responses
- rush your answers
- be intimidated
- criticize or speak negatively of previous experiences
- make excuses

WHEN IT'S YOUR TURN

Depending upon the interview structure and format, you may not have the opportunity to ask questions of your own until the interview is nearly finished. Although interviewers expect that you will have some questions to ask of them, not all will set aside time for this purpose. Even those who do invite questions

73

often wait until they have covered all of the topics they consider most important. It is natural that you will formulate questions during the course of the interview, but you should also have prepared some general questions covering topics of special interest to you. The nature and timing of your questions will demonstrate that you have given some thought to the position, that you have listened attentively as the conversation progressed, and that you are sincerely interested in making the right decision. Questions can be used to clarify ambiguities or to gather information about topics not covered. Developing your questions in advance will help you to avoid two potentially negative or embarrassing possibilities—asking questions simply for the sake of asking questions or drawing a blank when the opportunity arises. Some questions from the following list may be appropriate in almost any interview situation:

- What type of laboratory/computer/research facilities are available?
- How many professional staff members are employed in this department?
- What is the size of the support staff (secretaries, technicians, etc.)?
- Is money budgeted for professional meetings and conferences?
- How will I be evaluated? how often?
- What is the relationship between the community and the organization/institution?
- What is the turnover rate in the department?
- Why is this position vacant?
- What type of student enrolls in this department?
- What is a typical class size?
- Does the department employ teaching assistants?
- Where do your students come from?
- What is the attrition rate?
- What is the makeup of the student body—ethnic, racial, handicapped?
- Are there any typical assignments not specifically mentioned in the job description?
- Is summer teaching available?
- How many students receive financial assistance?
- Are support services available for students (counseling, career planning and placement, advising, etc.)?
- Is funding for this position dependent upon outside money (grants, etc.)?

- What is the salary range for this position?
- What is the total compensation package (retirement plan, insurance, etc.)?
- When do you expect to make a decision?
- How will I be notified?

END ON A POSITIVE NOTE

Typically, it is the responsibility of the interviewer to bring the conversation to a close. If you are engaged in a series of interviews, however, you do have some responsibility to try to stay on schedule. While you cannot dictate the length of a conversation, you may exert some control by tactfully indicating that you have another person waiting to see you. In such cases, however, the interviewer generally will be aware of your schedule and will try to conclude the session within the allotted time. You need to be perceptive to cues that the conversation is drawing to a conclusion, but before leaving an interview you should know when a decision will be made and how you will be contacted. You also need to know if there is anything else required of you. If these issues are not clearly explained, be sure to ask the appropriate questions. Do not prolong the interview, but try to make your final statement as impressive as your first. A positive expression of your interest in the position and a comment that your interest has deepened on the basis of the interview is always in order—if it is true. Regardless of your feelings about the position, you should, as a professional courtesy, express appreciation for the interview.

EVALUATING YOUR INTERVIEW PERFORMANCE

In spite of the release of tension and natural post-interview relief, resist the temptation to consider the interview complete. No interview is complete without your evaluation. Whether you are waiting in a campus lounge, motel room, or airport terminal, the period immediately following the interview should be used productively. While everything is fresh in your mind, try to make some notes about important topics covered and be sure to jot down items that should have been discussed or questions you should have asked but didn't because there was insufficient time or because you simply forgot.

This is not the time to speculate on your chances of being hired. Incorrect speculations can lead to greater disappointments and letdowns and may affect your preparation and performance at future interviews. You cannot compare yourself with other candidates interviewed; nor can you know all the factors that influence the ultimate selection of the person to be hired. Consequently, it is pointless to attempt predictions. The only speculation you should make is whether you would accept the position if offered.

The post-interview evaluation period should be a time for positive retrospection. Being overly critical of yourself or of the interviewer serves no useful purpose and results in a loss of objectivity. One of the easiest things for you to evaluate is your response to specific questions. If you stumbled or could not come up with a satisfactory answer, focus your attention on these problem areas before your next interview. Also think about those questions you answered well. Note your responses and hope that you will be asked similar questions in future interviews.

Reflecting on how you conducted yourself during social functions should also be a priority in a post-interview evaluation. Group functions in interview situations may never be easy, but you should be more relaxed the second time around. Many of your reactions will depend upon your hosts. If they take the initiative to introduce you to others and to make sure that you feel comfortable, social functions are more manageable than if you are left to circulate on your own. You should not depend on your host to act as a liaison, however. Be prepared to strike out on your own, to introduce yourself, and to chat with as many guests as possible.

FOLLOWING THROUGH

After the interview, a letter expressing your continued interest or withdrawing your name from the list of finalists must be sent to the appropriate individual (head of the search committee, department chair, director, president, etc.). Your letter can be relatively brief and to the point. If you were asked to provide additional materials or documents, they may be enclosed with your letter or you may state they are being forwarded by the appropriate office or agency. Your letter can reinforce topics discussed or introduce relevant material that was not adequately covered during the interview. Finally, but not necessarily least important, the letter demonstrates that you understand and practice professional courtesies. For an example of an interview follow-up letter, see page 56.

After you have written your follow-up letter and submitted any necessary papers or documents, you must be prepared for a waiting period while the search committee or hiring official arrives at a decision about your candidacy. Keep in mind that timelines established during your interview are not always exact. If you were informed that you would be contacted within two weeks you should not be surprised if at least three weeks go by without a letter or telephone call. Do not, however, let this waiting period drag on indefinitely; a telephone call to the hiring official inquiring about the status of your candidacy is appropriate. Unexpected developments may have delayed the decision and your inquiry will at least let you know when a decision is anticipated.

You must, of course, be prepared to learn that a decision has been made and that you were not the person selected for the position. In either case, your comments must be professional and tactful. Disappointment at not being selected is a natural reaction and you need not try to conceal it from the hiring official. You may, however, express your regret and indicate that you would appreciate being considered for any similar position that might become available.

CONSIDERING OFFERS AND MAKING DECISIONS

The final component of any job search is accepting an offer of employment. Simple as this seems, every job seeker needs to be aware that offers can be extended in different ways and that there are many decisions to be made before an offer should be accepted. Receiving an offer marks the culmination of your efforts; it can also spur a brief but intense period of soul-searching as well as celebration. For most academics and professionals the decision to accept or reject an offer of employment has far-reaching consequences. Accepting the offer represents both a legal and ethical commitment that should not be entered into without careful consideration of the impact of the decision on your immediate plans and your future objectives.

When you are selected for a position, you may be notified of the offer in person, by telephone, or by mail. Depending upon the position and the organization offering employment, you may be required only to make a verbal commitment, or you may be asked to sign either a letter of appointment or a contract. Employment offers always require a response and typically indicate a deadline for your acceptance. Although deadlines can vary from twenty-four hours to ten days or perhaps even a month, you should respond as soon as you are able. If only a verbal commitment is required it is essential that you confirm your acceptance with a letter outlining the terms of the agreement, such as responsibilities, salary, and starting date. (See the sample letter of acceptance on page 58.) Should you be asked to sign a formal document, either retain one of the copies or make a photocopy for your records.

Once you receive an offer of employment, there are a number of personal and professional items that you will want to address. Consideration of the following questions may influence your decision to accept or decline an offer.

- Is this the kind of job I want?
- How closely do the responsibilities and duties of this position match my interests and background?
- Can I work cooperatively with other staff/faculty members and with the administration?

77

- Are my expectations appropriate for the students enrolled at this institution?
- Is my philosophy compatible with that of the organization/institution?
- Are research facilities adequate and accessible?
- Are salary and other benefits satisfactory?
- Is the organization/institution financially sound?

You will also need to consider the effects of the offered position on your career by attempting to answer the following questions:

- Will I be working in my area of expertise?
- Does the position offer job security/tenure possibilities?
- Is there opportunity for advancement/promotion?
- Is the job a dead end?
- Could this position be a stepping-stone to a better job?
- Is the organization/institution reputable?
- Can I find personal as well as professional satisfaction in the job?

The position, the terms of appointment, and the institution or organization are primary considerations for everyone. But if you receive more than one offer, or if you must consider the needs and desires of other family members, the features of the community must also be evaluated. Questions you will need to consider might include:

- Is the relationship between the institution and the community satisfactory?
- Is housing available and affordable?
- Is transportation/commuting a problem?
- Are there employment or educational opportunities for my spouse?
- Are there satisfactory day-care facilities/schools for my children?
- Do community recreational and cultural resources meet my needs?

Reviewing the impressions of the community you formed during your interview visit will help you to answer some of these questions. If additional information about the community is desired, it can be obtained easily and quickly by contacting the community's Chamber of Commerce. Most Chambers of Commerce will be happy to send maps, promotional brochures, or pamphlets describing the resources of their community. Beneath the propaganda there are facts about the schools, taxes, housing, major industries, transportation, libraries, theaters, recreational facilities, etc. If time has not allowed you to gather this type of information before your interview, you will want to do so as soon as possible after your return so that if you are offered the position you will have sufficient knowledge of the community to make a sound decision.

Job seekers who anticipate or receive more than one offer of employment will find the various questions related to the position and community useful for comparison purposes before arriving at a decision. If you have followed through with your post-interview evaluations, you have probably already determined the priority of different opportunities. Your decision can be made quickly and without much difficulty if the offer is from your preferred institution or organization. However, if you receive an offer from an employer who is not your first choice, it is advisable to contact hiring officials at the preferred organization to inform them that an offer has been extended to you and to inquire about the status of your candidacy. In order to make the best decision, you must determine if you are still under consideration and when a decision is expected. Based on this information, you can arrive at a decision to accept or decline your first offer. In most instances, you should be able to make your decision within the allotted time, but if this is not possible you can request an extension. Additional time must be requested only in exceptional circumstances. Extensions should be requested in a telephone conversation with the hiring official and confirmed in writing. Once you have committed yourself to accepting a position, it is a professional courtesy to inform the other search committees or hiring officials of your decision.

Chapter Five

Options and Obstacles: Special Considerations in Your Job Search

With minor variations, the application and selection processes outlined in preceding chapters are nearly universal; job seekers, however, are not so easily defined. Each person approaches the employment process with a unique background and with particular requirements, preferences, priorities, and expectations. Traditionally, a successful job search is one that culminates with an offer of a full-time position. More recently, because of an overcrowded market and financial constraints imposed on higher education and on federal, state, and local agencies, many Ph.D.'s and M.A.'s have come to realize that no job offering personal and professional rewards can be overlooked or underestimated. Employment options discussed in this chapter can help you to recognize academic opportunities that may not have occurred to you but that can permit you to secure employment and to gain valuable experience in your field.

TEMPORARY ACADEMIC EMPLOYMENT

Most academics consider temporary employment as a matter of necessity, not of choice. Temporary positions can range from one-semester replacements for faculty members on sabbatical leave to fixed-term appointments of one to three years' duration. Because, in many fields, there are more qualified people than available jobs, temporary appointments should not be viewed as inferior in quality or merit. Unstable funding, fluctuating enrollments, and heavily tenured departments in most colleges and universities make it inevitable that some people begin their careers in temporary appointments.

ADVANTAGES OF TAKING A TEMPORARY POSITION

If you are a first-time job seeker, your selection for a temporary position should bolster your self-confidence and assure you that you are conducting your job search properly and effectively. Gaining experience in your field will usually make it easier for you to find your next job because you will have demonstrated that you are employable. Even though the position is temporary, the opportunity to teach in your chosen field and to work on a professional level with colleagues and students is beneficial. In addition, you will undoubtedly gain perspective on the way departments and colleges operate and you may well gain insight into the selection process. While employed, it is easier for you to extend your network of contacts who can be instrumental in helping you to find the permanent employment you desire.

PROBLEMS OF THE PERIPATETIC PROFESSOR

Continued temporary employment usually implies a nomadic existence—moving from one job to another and constantly searching for a new position. It is difficult to channel your energies into your assigned duties when you must constantly seek employment opportunities, write letters of application, and prepare for interviews. At the same time, you are faced with meeting new students and colleagues, new neighbors, exploring an unfamiliar community, and perhaps helping your family become oriented to a new location. The combination of trying to settle into a new job while you are continuing your search for another can drain personal and professional energies. For most people, this creates a feeling of being in limbo and can severely inhibit the ability to concentrate on scholarship and professional activities. With little or no chance for a permanent appointment in your present location, you may lack the incentive to be active in your department or even in your discipline through writing papers or making presentations at professional conferences—even though common sense tells you that these activities should be undertaken in order to make you more competitive for other vacancies. As a temporary member of a department, you may feel that you are on the fringes of the group without real opportunity to contribute as fully as you might wish. This perception of yourself as an outsider can affect your relationships with your colleagues and can interfere with the ability to develop meaningful friendships. These problems can be distracting enough in any one situation, but a succession of temporary appointments multiplies and intensifies the feeling of alienation.

Another danger of successive temporary appointments is that you will be labeled a gypsy scholar. Potential employers may begin to wonder why you have found only short-term positions or why you have not been retained at one of your previous jobs. Even though most employers try to be sensitive to the plight of younger scholars, and they do know that there are simply not enough full-time tenure-track jobs to go around, a series of temporary jobs can raise questions and doubts in the minds of selection committees. Perhaps an even greater danger is that your awareness of these considerations coupled with the uprooting and traumatic effects of constantly being in the middle of a job search can begin to erode your own self-confidence.

Seeking a new position every year or two makes it imperative that you present your temporary employment accurately and positively. If your position was designated "Visiting Assistant Professor" or if you were replacing a faculty member on sabbatical leave, this should be clearly stated. In other situations, you may need to include in your description of the position such phrases as "position was dependent on outside funding which was not renewed" or "position eliminated due to declining enrollment." Even though you must revise your vita each year or perhaps even more often, do not make the mistake of attempting to update it by squeezing in your most recent experience or writing in changes of address or teaching interests. Take the time to do a thorough, professional job of producing a clean, updated vita for each job search. In most cases it is crucial to arrange the information in such a way that the position and its responsibilities, and not the dates of employment, receive the emphasis. Compare the samples below and notice how the second grouping emphasizes the position and minimizes the term of the appointment.

Traditional setup:

TEACHING EXPERIENCE

| 1977-78 | Sabbatical Replacement for Professor of Economics
Loma Linda University, Riverside, California |
| 1978-80 | Visiting Assistant Professor of Economics
Northwestern University, Evanston, Illinois |

Position-oriented setup:

TEACHING EXPERIENCE

Sabbatical Replacement for Professor of Economics, 1977-78
Loma Linda University, Riverside, California

Visiting Assistant Professor of Economics, 1978-80
Northwestern University, Evanston, Illinois

At the interview stage of your job search, you must convey a positive attitude about your various work experiences, emphasizing the responsibilities and the opportunity to experience a variety of settings, students, and colleagues. As in any communication with employers, you may need to reinforce the fact that your positions were temporary and that you were not fired or forced to resign.

PART-TIME EMPLOYMENT

Some Ph.D.'s and M.A.'s investigate part-time job opportunities only after conducting an exhaustive but fruitless search for full-time positions. If economic circumstances dictate that you work full-time to support yourself and your family, you may eventually be forced to take a non-related job while you continue to look for more suitable employment. In the meantime, part-time jobs can allow you to remain active in your field and perhaps enhance your qualifications for future full-time opportunities. Some job seekers may, indeed, seek part-time employment as a first choice. Reasons for this decision will vary with each individual, but typical reasons for preferring a part-time job may include family responsibilities, the desire to pursue creative activities, such as writing or painting, or to concentrate on other personal interests or, in the case of academics, the need for time to take additional courses or to complete a dissertation.

Whatever its advantages, part-time employment has drawbacks, too. If the job depends upon enrollment or outside funding, hiring may be delayed until the last moment, allowing little time for advance preparation. Furthermore, you cannot depend upon such jobs continuing beyond the present term. Even in a continuing part-time position there is little opportunity for promotion or tenure in the case of academic jobs. Salaries for part-time employees are often less than equivalent to the amount you would receive for comparable work in a full-time position, and benefits may be limited or simply not offered. There is also the possibility that you may be labeled a part-timer by your employer. Some departments or agencies may find your services as a part-time employee so valuable that they prefer to hire someone else for a new position and to retain you on a part-time basis. This can be especially true if you are restricted to a certain community.

Whether choice or necessity is responsible for your decision to secure part-time employment related to your career goals, you should be aware of the various types of part-time positions typically available. In both the public and private sectors, financial considerations and the demand for professional services create part-time opportunities for advanced degree holders in almost every field.

Saturday and Evening Class Programs. To accommodate students who are unable to attend classes during the day, colleges and universities may offer Saturday and evening courses. The number of contact hours approximates the amount of time spent teaching a typical class during regular daytime hours, but is concentrated into one or two weekly meetings. Students in Saturday and evening class programs often represent a combination of regular full-time students who register for these courses because of schedule conflicts or work or family obligations and nontraditional students who prefer or can only arrange to take classes at times other than the normal school day. Contact the office responsible for scheduling Saturday and evening class programs to inquire about employment possibilities.

Overflow Classes. When enrollments exceed expectations, instructors may be needed for basic or required courses. These positions are usually available on a term-by-term basis and the need for additional sections may not be determined until registration has been completed. In some cases, this may mean that the need is not known until classes have begun. Direct contact with the department can be initiated early, but it is essential to maintain contact during the time immediately preceding the opening of classes.

Weekend Colleges. Some campuses have established weekend degree programs to meet the needs of students who are employed or otherwise unable to attend classes during the week. The size and nature of the program will determine the need for additional faculty members. Smaller programs may employ current faculty for these weekend courses; comprehensive weekend degree programs may employ a parallel faculty specifically for weekend students. The method of instruction is similar to that of a typical college course, but contact hours are concentrated into one or two days. Most often, students are expected to cover the same amount of material, to complete similar assignments, and to write examinations comparable to those required in traditional weekday classes. To identify colleges and universities offering weekend degree programs, consult *Who Offers Part-Time Degree Programs?* (Peterson's Guides).

Correspondence Courses. Correspondence courses are offered by many colleges and universities on a year-round basis. Students can enroll in correspondence courses for academic credit at any time during the year and usually must complete the course within one year of enrollment. Instructors may be responsible for designing curriculum materials, grading assignments and papers, and preparing and evaluating examinations. Many instructors are faculty members or advanced graduate students but there are opportunities for part-time work. To identify accredited colleges offering correspondence courses, consult Peterson's *The Independent Study Catalog.* To check on employment opportunities, contact the college or university office handling correspondence studies.

Media Studies. Many colleges and universities offer courses through a variety of media, ranging from audio-conferencing, live classroom microwave television, radio and television broadcasts, to newspaper courses. Audio-conferencing and microwave television courses offer two-way communication between the students and the instructor. For example, The University of Iowa's Telebridge courses allow the instructors to conduct classes from their offices utilizing microphones attached to their telephones. Contact time and expectations are similar to or identical with regular classroom teaching. Students may be expected to view or listen to lectures, participate in discussions, and to study materials the instructor sends for the class to review. Typically, courses are taught by regular faculty members, but advanced degree holders can inquire about the possibility of part-time teaching opportunities. Contact the continuing education or extension division to inquire about courses offered and class schedules.

Off-Campus or Outreach Programs. As an alternative to traditional, on-campus full-time study, courses are offered at sites located outside the university community. Credits may be earned through undergraduate or graduate study programs, inservice training sessions, or professional development seminars. Instructors for off-campus programs are often faculty or professional staff of the college or university offering the programs, but opportunities exist for Ph.D.'s and M.A.'s with appropriate qualifications. Contact the university or college office responsible for off-campus or outreach programs to inquire about employment possibilities.

Noncredit Programs. Noncredit courses designed to promote personal growth and development may be offered on college campuses, in high schools, or in community learning centers. Courses are usually conducted in an informal atmosphere, grades are not assigned, tests are not required, and no academic credit is earned. There are no admission requirements for students other than an interest in learning, and courses may range from leisure interests such as bridge classes to music appreciation to computer literacy courses. Classes are usually conducted in evening sessions ranging from one to three hours over a period of four to six weeks. Contact your local college or university to inquire about their noncredit programs. The public library is a good source of information about community education programs.

Academic and Special-Interest Camps. During the summer, many colleges and universities offer specialized learning sessions in such diverse areas as sports, music, drama, dance, science, computers, and outdoor education. Most of the "camps" are designed to introduce students to new interests or to develop and refine skills in a particular field. Programs are organized for age groups ranging from adolescents to adults. Instructors and counselors are hired to work with students individually and in group settings. The camps may be located on college campuses or in settings appropriate to the field of study, such as science camps based in wilderness areas. A well-known summer program designed to assist minorities and disadvantaged youth planning to attend college is the Upward Bound program. Elderhostel programs are designed for persons over sixty and their spouses, offering noncredit courses often adapted from classes offered during the regular academic term, but without requiring outside assignments or examinations. To inquire about employment possibilities in academic and special-interest camps, contact local colleges and specific programs. Further information about the Elderhostel program may be requested from: Elderhostel National Registration Office, 100 Boylston Street, Suite 200, Boston, MA 02116.

DUAL CAREERS

For many years it was assumed that one member of the household (usually the husband) would be fully employed outside the home and that the marriage partner (usually the wife) would subordinate career goals and interests to other responsibilities (housekeeping, parenting, social obligations). Only in recent times have dual careers become feasible, socially acceptable, and—in many cases—an economic necessity. Today it is no longer assumed that one partner's career will be relegated to an inferior position. If you are married, engaged, or involved in a serious relationship with another person, it is highly unlikely that your job search can be conducted without consideration for your partner's career development.

If each of you is seeking a career in a separate field, the marketability of each degree must be evaluated. If one of you is likely to have a greater possibility for employment, you need to decide whether to place greater emphasis on the easier job search or on the one you expect to be more difficult. There may be good reasons for either option, but some of the advantages of concentrating on the job search of the person with more or better opportunities are: a greater chance of finding a position in a preferred location, less anxiety if you can be assured that at least one of you will have gainful employment, and perhaps a shorter and less intensive job search for the first position. Once one of you has located a position, the other can concentrate job-seeking efforts on that particular geographic area. On the other hand, if the person with the less marketable degree wants to pursue a full-scale job search, the other partner may have greater probability of finding professional employment in the same area. Before deciding which partner's job search will take precedence, serious consideration should be given to the question of which partner would better adapt to or tolerate unemployment or part-time employment at least on a temporary basis. However, if the expected earnings are significantly different, it may be advisable to concentrate your efforts on the job search of the partner who can earn the higher salary.

If job opportunities for each partner appear to be approximately equal and both of you are interested in conducting a full-scale job search, it is advantageous to do so. But before employment plans and job-seeking strategies can be developed, you and your partner must consider and discuss the following questions:

- Is daily commuting possible for one of you? both of you?
- Are you willing to consider living apart?
- Is weekend long-distance commuting economically feasible?

In dual career situations, each partner conducts an independent job search. Even if you and your partner are applying for positions in the same field, at the same institution—even for the same position—you will write individual letters and submit individual vitas. The only instance in which your efforts can be combined is if the two of you decide to seek a joint appointment.

JOINT APPOINTMENTS OR JOB SHARING

Another employment possibility for partners with degrees in the same field is to share the responsibilities of one academic or professional position. Some of the more common reasons for people to share a position may include equal participation in family obligations or child-rearing responsibilities while allowing each partner to be gainfully employed, to realize career goals and to gain professional experience, or to allow each partner time to pursue scholarly or creative endeavors. In order for job sharing to be feasible, the degrees must be roughly comparable and individual competencies or skills must be complementary. For example, if a music department needed someone to teach studio piano and music theory or history, this vacancy could be filled by one person with competencies in each area or by two individuals with highly specialized backgrounds. Two people with the same academic backgrounds and qualifications could also share one appointment by alternating days or dividing up courses between them. Rarely if ever will an employer deliberately seek two people for one position. However, even if a vacancy is not advertised as a joint appointment, it is certainly possible for two people to apply for the job.

Employers usually benefit from joint appointments in several ways. No matter how the responsibilities of the position may be divided (50-50, 60-40, or alternating terms), each partner usually devotes more time than is required or even expected. For example, in an academic setting, students receive the benefit of more than one teaching style and often receive more individual attention than one instructor could provide. A partnership may also benefit the department through individual involvement or participation in committee assignments or other activities. Because two individuals share one appointment, the employer receives the skills and commitment of two professionals for the price of one.

Preparing for a job search leading to a joint appointment involves special considerations. Each partner must be equally supportive of the decision and must have agreed, for whatever reason, that a joint appointment offers the best possible employment opportunity. In order to be successful in a joint appointment, each person must be committed to the decision and to the responsibilities. Each partner must be capable of articulating the reason for choosing to share a position and of convincing a potential employer that the two of you can offer more than a single candidate. Applying for a joint appointment involves a marketing strategy that presents you as a team but allows each partner to accent individual strengths and competencies. The first step in the search for a joint appointment or shared position is the same as it would be for an independent job search—each partner develops an individual vita presenting academic background and professional qualifications. A joint vita is neither necessary nor generally advisable for the simple reason that it can be too long, too cumbersome, and too confusing. Cover letters, including letters of inquiry and application, should be joint efforts. The sample letter illustrates how to apply for a joint appointment.

If you are invited to interview for a joint appointment, travel allowances may not be sufficient to cover expenses for both partners. As with any travel arrangements, information must be obtained in advance, but you should not be surprised if the employing institution offers expenses for only one person since the interview is for one position.

Applicants for joint appointments can expect to be interviewed as a team but it is also quite likely that each partner may be interviewed individually by the search committee or designated members of the committee. Some special questions about your working relationship and joint responsibilities should be anticipated:

- Why are you seeking a joint appointment?
- Have you attempted collaborative efforts before?
- What is the strongest asset the two of you can bring to our organization?
- How will your team approach benefit our students or clients?
- Do you intend to make a career of joint appointments?
- Can you identify any drawbacks or negative aspects of sharing one position?
- What if one partner should decide to leave?
- How would each of you handle student or subordinate complaints about the other?
- What if I want to hire only one of you?
- What if it should become necessary to release one of you?

For any interview, time and effort are required in preparation, but joint interviews demand additional thought and planning. Each partner must know individual and team strengths and weaknesses, and must be capable of contributing equally to the conversation. If one partner appears to dominate the interview, the image of a professional partnership is diminished. It is also important for individual responses to be consistent with each other and with the image presented jointly through previous correspondence. Throughout the entire selection process,

SAMPLE LETTER OF JOINT APPLICATION

1968 Brandt Place
Lawrence, Kansas 66045
April 1, 1984

Karen Sorensen
Chair, Department of Theatre Arts
Baylor University
Waco, Texas 76798

Dear Professor Sorensen:

We are submitting our joint application for the position of Assistant Professor of Acting and Directing advertised in the March edition of the National Arts Jobbank. The enclosed vitae summarize our academic and professional qualifications and experiences. You will note that we have each completed the terminal degree in our area of specialization.

We believe our combined strengths in acting and directing can offer your students greater depth in each area than one full-time person could provide. We propose to divide the responsibilities of the position in the following manner: Janee Nelson would teach the introductory and advanced acting courses; David Dettmann would teach the direction sequence and be responsible for directing the two productions each year. We are both interested in advising students and have considerable experience in academic theatre as well as in semi-professional and professional theatre. We feel that our expertise and enthusiasm could bring to your program a unique combination of professional skills and backgrounds.

We are very excited about the possibility of joining your department and would welcome the opportunity to discuss the position with you. We plan to attend the American Educational Theatre Association conference in Anaheim and would be happy to meet with you then or to visit your campus at any time. Our dossiers are being forwarded to you and if we can provide any additional information please contact us.

Sincerely yours,

Janee Nelson

Janee Nelson

David Dettmann

David Dettmann

Encs.

and perhaps most obviously at the interview, it is important that each partner convey the image of a highly competent, skilled individual who is committed to working in a joint appointment.

REENTERING THE JOB MARKET

If you have been working outside your field, if you have interrupted your career for family responsibilities, or if you have simply been unemployed, once you decide to reenter the job market there are special considerations of which you must be aware. Having been outside academic and professional circles need not prevent you from finding suitable employment, but in order to arrive at realistic predictions of your chances for successful reentry there are many factors which must be assessed. Your chances for a successful job campaign will be influenced by the number of years you have been away from your field, your previous employment record, your involvement and demonstrated interest in your profession since your last job or your last degree, your reasons for "dropping out," the current competition for jobs in your area, your age, your mobility, flexibility, and your expectations. Finally, your ability to market yourself cannot be discounted.

UPDATING YOURSELF

If you conclude that you can be competitive for part-time or full-time positions in your field, then you should consider investing the time and money necessary to reenter your profession. Selling yourself to potential employers necessitates your presenting a professional image worthy of their consideration and capable of stimulating their interest. In order to create the desired image, you must be familiar with recent trends in your field, including current research, theories, writings, or practices. Renewing memberships in professional associations, reading professional journals, or attending professional conferences will be essential if you have not remained professionally active or if you have not had the opportunity to remain in contact with colleagues. In conjunction with updating knowledge of your field, you must make an effort to familiarize yourself with current economic, social, and political issues as they relate to the type of employment you seek. The *Chronicle of Higher Education,* for example, not only lists information about job opportunities, but also provides a good sense of contemporary issues and attitudes on college and university campuses and acquaints you with the concerns of today's students, faculty, and administrators. Visiting college campuses can help orient you to the social environment and general mood of current students.

UPDATING PROFESSIONAL MATERIALS

If you have been out of the market for some time, getting your professional materials organized and updated will not be dissimilar to starting a new job search. If you had a placement file at your college or university, contact the placement office to inquire about procedures for updating and reactivating your dossier. Some offices retain inactive files indefinitely; others discard inactive files after a period of several years. In any event, your dossier will need to be updated to meet your present needs and to reflect your current objectives. Older references which may no longer be relevant should be deleted, although references pertaining to professional experience are important to most employers even if they are not recent and should probably be retained. You may find it desirable or essential to add new references. Recommendations regarding professional nonrelated employment or even volunteer activities can be appropriate additions. If you have maintained contact with some of the people who previously submitted recommendations for your file, it can be to your advantage to request a new statement but it is neither appropriate nor necessary to obtain current recommendations from all former employers. In most cases, the older reference will be more specific and detailed than a new statement can be.

You may have in your personal files a copy of the vita you used for your previous job searches. Some vitas can simply be updated; others must be completely revised. Regardless of the extent of revision required, the vita must always be retyped. Even to meet a deadline, it is inappropriate to squeeze additional information into an existing copy or to make handwritten corrections. A total overhaul will undoubtedly be necessary if you have been away from your field for several years or have had numerous experiences in the interim.

To illustrate methods of revising a vita, let us take Denise Overman's vita from Chapter 3 and project it into the future. If Denise has not been employed in her field for several years, the basic format can remain the same but she may need to rearrange or modify some of the information appearing on the vita she prepared for her earlier job search. Categories have been rearranged to place greater emphasis on teaching interests and teaching experience by presenting them first. Because the doctorate remains a primary qualification for an academic position, this information remains fairly prominent. Even though it has been some time since Denise worked under the direction of her dissertation adviser, she has retained his name because of his international reputation. The dates have been moved to the end of each entry in an effort to maximize the experience and qualifications and to minimize the chronology. In the "Honors" category, dates have been deleted. Because of the rapid changes in her field, research interests are not identified. Additions to the "Publications" and "Service" categories indicate that Denise has remained interested and active in her discipline. Although there are no changes in the entries listed under "Memberships," the revised vita

SAMPLE VITA

DENISE OVERMAN

ADDRESSES:	Home:	Office:
	429 Oak Street	204 Chemistry Building
	Apt. #421B	Purdue University
	Lafayette, Indiana 47906	West Lafayette, Indiana 47907
	(317) 555-2664	(317) 494-4000

EDUCATION:

1983 Ph.D., Purdue University, West Lafayette, Indiana
Physical Chemistry
    Dissertation topic: Crystal structures of several
    intermetallic compounds of gadolinium and
    dyprosium with manganese and iron.
Dr. G. W. Terhune, adviser

1975 M.A., University of Minnesota, Minneapolis, Minnesota
Chemistry

1973 B.A., Cornell College, Mt. Vernon, Iowa
Chemistry/Physics

HONORS:

1981-83 National Science Foundation Fellow, Purdue Univ.
1974 John Upson Fellowship, University of Minnesota
1972-73 Martin-Merriwether Scholarship, Cornell College
1969-73 Dean's list (7 semesters), Cornell College

TEACHING EXPERIENCE:

1981-83 Teaching Assistant, Purdue University
    General Chemistry, Physical Chemistry
1975-77 Chemistry Instructor, Augsburg College, Minneapolis,
    Minnesota

RELATED EXPERIENCE:

1977-79 Industrial Researcher, Monsanto Company, St. Louis,
    Missouri
1974 Summer Technical Assistant, 3M Company, St. Paul,
    Minnesota

TEACHING INTERESTS: Undergraduate courses in physical and organic chemistry;
graduate courses in physical chemistry

RESEARCH INTERESTS: Determination of molecular structure of biologically important
compounds using X-ray diffraction
Techniques of neutron diffraction

PUBLICATION: "Structure of Uranium Dicarbide Determined by Neutron
Diffraction," D. Overman and J. Hart, *Journal of Chemical
Physics,* 42, 282, 1982.

MEMBERSHIPS: Phi Beta Kappa
Alpha Chi Sigma
Phi Lambda Upsilon
American Chemical Society

SERVICE: Departmental Undergraduate Curriculum Committee, 1981-82
Student Member, Search Committee for Dean of Graduate
School, 1981
Secretary, Graduate Student Association, 1980-81

CREDENTIALS: Educational Placement, Matthews Hall, Purdue University,
West Lafayette, Indiana 47907 (317) 494-3990

REVISED VITA

DENISE OVERMAN

ADDRESS:	2 Center Avenue, Lafayette, Indiana 47906 (317) 555-2664
TEACHING INTERESTS:	Undergraduate courses in physical and organic chemistry; graduate courses in physical chemistry
TEACHING EXPERIENCE:	Teaching Assistant, Purdue University, 1981-83 General Chemistry, Physical Chemistry Chemistry Instructor, Augsburg College, Minneapolis, Minnesota, 1975-77
RELATED EXPERIENCE:	Industrial Researcher, Monsanto Company, St. Louis, Missouri, 1977-79 Summer Technical Assistant, 3M Company, St. Paul, Minnesota, 1974
EDUCATION:	Ph.D., Purdue University, West Lafayette, Indiana, 1983 Physical Chemistry Dissertation topic: Crystal structures of several intermetallic compounds of gadolinium and dyprosium with manganese and iron. Dr. G. W. Terhune, advisor M.A., University of Minnesota, Minneapolis, Minnestoa, 1975 Chemistry B.A., Cornell College, Mt. Vernon, Iowa, 1973 Chemistry/Physics
HONORS:	National Science Foundation Fellow, Purdue University John Upson Fellowship, University of Minnesota Martin-Merriwether Scholarship, Cornell College Dean's list (7 semesters), Cornell College
PUBLICATIONS:	"Career Interruptions and How They Work," Point of View article for *The Chronicle of Higher Education,* XXX, 6, October 13, 1984. "Structure of Uranium Dicarbide Determined by Neutron Diffraction," D. Overman and J. Hart, *Journal of Chemical Physics,* 42, 282, 1982.
SERVICE:	Reader for the *Purdue Science Newsletter,* 1983 to present Departmental Undergraduate Curriculum Committee, 1981-82 Student Member, Search Committee for Dean of Graduate School, 1981
CURRENT MEMBERSHIPS:	Phi Beta Kappa Alpha Chi Sigma Phi Lambda Upsilon American Chemical Society
CREDENTIALS:	Educational Placement, Matthews Hall, Purdue University, West Lafayette, Indiana 47907 (317) 494-3990

uses the category heading "Current Memberships" to stress continued involvement in the organizations.

Cover letters accompanying your revised vita must also concentrate on your current employment objective, your strengths, abilities, and qualifications. There is no need to draw attention to the fact that you have not been employed in your field for some time. Eliminate irrelevancies; you are not writing your confessions or your memoirs. No apologies are necessary nor is this the place to justify your absence from your profession.

UPDATING INTERVIEWING SKILLS

Individuals who have been away from their profession often find the interview situation even more stressful than the first-time job seeker. While it is not possible to alleviate all anxiety, a few preliminary steps can help to keep the stress at a manageable level. In addition to the things that any job seeker must know about the position, the institution, and the community, you can anticipate questions pertaining to your particular situation, such as:

- What has prompted you to return to your field?
- How have you kept in touch with developments in your field?
- What can you offer our department and our students/clients at this point in your career?
- What differences do you anticipate between today's students and those you previously taught?
- In resuming your career at this point in your life, what are your goals?

Not all of these questions will be asked directly, but they should be anticipated and your responses should answer the unspoken questions as well. There is no doubt that people seeking to reenter their profession are often at a disadvantage. If you have been invited to interview, you can be encouraged by the fact that you have already overcome some of the obstacles and that you are considered a competitive candidate. To remain one of the top candidates, you must appear confident, enthusiastic, and, above all, committed to your profession and to your place in it.

CONFRONTING EMPLOYMENT OBSTACLES

For some individuals, the problem of finding satisfactory employment is compounded by circumstances which do not relate to their qualifications, abilities, or potential. If you have any special condition or circumstance that a hiring official might perceive as an obstacle to your employment, your recognition of employer attitudes and concerns can help you to confront some of the barriers you may encounter. Your ability to deal effectively with these special considerations and to present a confident professional image in any employment situation can have a direct effect on your current job search and the future direction of your career.

IF YOU HAVE A HANDICAP

Although a handicap is not necessarily a barrier to finding satisfactory employment, individuals with physical impairments or limitations face two special considerations in the job search. First, you must consider the accessibility of the campus or other facility and the community as a whole. Second, you must decide whether or not to inform the employer of your condition. In recent years, many campuses and office buildings have made special efforts to accommodate disabled individuals, but some communities have made no provisions for persons with ambulatory problems. Whether you are applying for a job at a college or in the private sector, you may obtain accurate information about campus and community facilities and accessibility by contacting the campus office responsible for assisting students with physical handicaps. The Association on Handicapped Student Service Programs in Postsecondary Education publishes an annual membership directory available from the Executive Director, AHSSPPE, P.O. Box 21192, Ohio State University, Columbus, Ohio 43221.

Raising the Issue

The question of when or how to inform a potential employer of a physical impairment creates doubts, uncertainties, and stress for most disabled job seekers. There is no one solution to this problem. If you have an obvious physical impairment, you have the choice of informing the prospective employer of your handicap in the initial application stages or during the interview. If you choose to inform potential employers of your condition in the early stages of the application process, you may refer to it on your vita or in your letter of application. Some individuals are more comfortable listing this information on the vita or including it in a letter of application so that the employer is aware of the condition before the interview stage of the selection process. Others prefer to wait until they have been selected for interviews before sharing this information with a prospective employer, either during the telephone conversation offering the interview or at the interview itself. Remember that only information relevant to your qualifications is essential on your vita or in your letter of application. You are not obligated to inform an employer of conditions which do not affect your ability to perform the duties and responsibilities of the position for which you are applying. Your decision in this matter should be one of personal choice.

Controlling the Discussion

In addition to the routine interview preparation required of any applicant, you will want to give some thought to the way in which you handle questions related to your impairment or the interviewer's avoidance of the subject. From your previous experiences, you know that some individuals find it difficult to relate to you as a person because of your handicap. You may recall that teachers, colleagues, and other acquaintances needed time to adjust to you and your physical condition. Employers, in most cases, will react just as any other new acquaintance. Some interviewers may be aware of the federal legislation on nondiscrimination on the basis of handicap (Section 504 of the Rehabilitation Act of 1973), but they may be uncomfortable about discussing your disability or even inquiring about it out of embarrassment, intimidation, or fear. They may be reluctant to appear to invade your privacy or they may be concerned about legal implications regarding discrimination in employment situations. Whatever their motivations for avoiding the issue, you need to be ready and willing to initiate and control any discussion related to your condition. The information you choose to provide should be offered openly and without hesitation, but remember that the focus of the interview must be on the job and your ability to handle it—not on your physical limitations. You should, of course, anticipate questions about the effect of your condition on your job performance:

- Are there any special accommodations you would require in your work station?
- In the past, how have your students or colleagues reacted to your handicap?
- Will your condition require constant medical attention?
- Will you need special assistance not routinely provided other staff members?
- Will additional funds be required to enable you to perform your duties?
- Do you anticipate any changes in your physical condition?

Perhaps the best way to handle questions about your condition is by illustration—for example, you might talk about your previous job or your experiences in graduate school. Your chances of being employed depend upon the employer receiving satisfactory answers to these questions—even though some of the questions may never be asked directly.

IF YOU ARE A CITIZEN OF ANOTHER COUNTRY

Foreign students who have completed an advanced degree and wish to seek employment in the United States must be aware that the job search will be affected by a number of special considerations. Although the actual process of finding a job is not significantly different for individuals who are not United States citizens or permanent residents, you might have some unique obstacles to overcome. As a graduate student, you are probably familiar with the tendency of students, and perhaps even professors, to see you first as a stereotype and second as an individual. Unfortunately, employers can be subject to the same limited perceptions. Although you may justifiably resent being stereotyped, if you recall your own anticipation of graduate study in the United States and your expectations of American people and their life-style, you will undoubtedly realize that stereotypes are the result of recurring impressions (largely created by the media) and insufficient firsthand experience.

Visa and Employment Regulations

If you obtained an F-1 student visa for the purpose of completing a graduate program, federal regulations concerning practical training state that you may remain in the United States to work for a period of not more than twelve months. If you wish to change to permanent resident status, you must secure an offer of permanent employment before a new visa can be issued. The employer must be willing to initiate and follow through with the necessary paperwork required by the U.S. Department of Labor and the Immigration and Naturalization Service before this change of status can be effected. These procedures cannot succeed unless the prospective employer can demonstrate that qualified U.S. citizens or permanent residents are not available to take the position the employer wishes to offer you. Because of the time involved and the chance that the change of status may not be approved, employers may be reluctant to give serious consideration to applications submitted by foreign students. It is easier to succeed in these procedures if you are offered a college or university teaching position than if you are offered some other kind of employment. For more information about procedures and requirements for changing to immigrant status, consult the National Association for Foreign Student Affairs' *Manual of Federal Regulations Affecting Foreign Students and Scholars.* To obtain a copy, contact a campus International Education Office or a foreign student adviser.

Anticipating Employer Concerns

Whether you intend to seek employment immediately or at some future time, a dossier should be assembled, references collected, and a vita prepared. If you are a permanent resident of the United States, your vita may include an additional category for this information and, if you completed part of your education in a non-English-speaking country, it may be to your advantage to indicate your ability to communicate effectively; for example, you may include a statement such as "read, write, and speak English fluently." Cover letters will, of course, demonstrate language proficiencies, but it is still advisable to include on the vita a statement attesting to your understanding of and fluency in English.

Your cover letter and vita will give the employer an idea of your writing skills, but the interview is of primary importance in demonstrating communication skills. In addition to verifying fluency and exchanging ideas about the position and its responsibilities, employers may use the interview to explore some of the following topics:

- reasons for seeking employment in the United States
- compatibility with colleagues
- cultural awareness
- knowledge of U.S. educational systems

Successful interviewing may depend upon your preparation and the thought you have given to conveying your responses positively, fluently, and honestly. Search committees are looking for individuals who are adaptable, flexible, and productive, and can represent their own culture and work harmoniously within the department, the institution, and the community.

IF YOU HAVE BEEN FIRED

The fact that you have been terminated from one position need not mean the end of your career, but the way you handle your dismissal does require special consideration. Your concern about the effect of being fired on future employment possibilities should focus on two distinct stages of the selection process—the application materials and the interview.

Employment History

Special thought must be given to your vita and dossier. As in any circumstance, it is best to tell the truth. You may be tempted to skip over or to delete the experience from your record, but it is not advisable to create gaps or to mislead potential employers about your work history. Employment of short duration could be an exception but, if you were employed for a year or more, omitting this information creates a gap that could raise questions. Of course, the vita and dossier must be consistent in stating where you have worked and the dates of your employment; it is never a good idea to omit the experience from one of these papers and to include it on another.

98

References

Your decision to request a reference from your previous employer or to apply for positions without one will be influenced by the length of the experience and the reasons for your release. It is generally to your professional advantage to have at least one reference from each relevant work experience; however, if you feel that a reference would be detrimental, it is probably best not to request one for your dossier. If you do request a reference, you should retain your right of access under the Family Educational Rights and Privacy Act of 1974 (the Buckley Amendment) so that you are aware of the nature and content of the statement. It is possible that a prospective employer will call your former supervisor, whether or not you have a statement in your dossier. This is a situation over which you have no control, but you should realize that the responses from your former supervisor may depend upon the type of questions asked. Many employers do not feel obligated to volunteer information beyond the scope of the inquiry. You should not assume that your previous employer's comments will always work against you. Although it is natural for you to feel some resentment or even personal animosity toward someone who has fired you, it can be a mistake to imagine that your previous employer holds the same feelings toward you. Depending upon the reasons for your termination, it may be that your former employer will recommend you for other jobs while explaining that you simply did not work out in that particular situation.

It is not unlikely that your department head or immediate supervisor will be contacted by one or more members of a selection committee either before or after your interview. Because academic and professional circles constitute relatively small worlds, it is never advisable to attempt to mislead or deceive a potential employer about your reasons for leaving a position. In most cases, you will be aware of the reasons for your release, and you should also be aware that potential employers will expect to discuss your previous work experience and your reasons for seeking a new job. Giving some prior thought to this issue can save embarrassment and discomfort at interviews and can help you avoid being eliminated from further consideration.

Be Positive

In anticipation of questions related to your employment record, you must be able to articulate your understanding of the situation, to relay information in the most positive manner possible, and to indicate that your enthusiasm and potential have not been diminished by an experience that did not prove mutually satisfactory. It may also be possible to demonstrate a recognition of the factors which led to your dismissal and to offer some assurance that altered conditions or personal growth will allow you to contribute productively in a new assignment.

Assuming that your academic preparation was not the issue, your dismissal probably came about because of errors in judgment, lack of professionalism, or personality traits.

The following phrases, though obviously not complete answers, can help you to develop your responses to questions about your previous experience:

- I realize now that I was being overly assertive.

- I was impatient with the bureaucracy.

- I wanted too much too soon.

- I was not emotionally prepared for my first job.

- I failed to recognize the importance of time management and setting priorities for my activities.

- I was naive about the political forces in the department.

- My personal situation at the time created problems and conflicts.

- It was an unfortunate conflict of personalities.

- It became apparent that there were serious philosophical differences between me and my supervisor.

- I had not learned to manage my portion of the budget and exceeded my allotment.

The tone and content of your responses must be positive and straightforward. Apologies and excuses are inappropriate and must be avoided. However you deal with your past experiences, it is important to recognize that you must help to direct the interview away from past problems and allow it to focus on your qualifications, your abilities, and your potential for success in the new assignment.

A job search immediately following a termination is never easy. Unless you allow a dismissal to dissuade you from pursuing your chosen career, however, it is entirely possible that you can, by presenting your qualifications and experiences as a professional, continue in your field.

Chapter Six

Expanding Your Options

You may know—or at least you have heard about—individuals who have successfully made a transition to employment in fields outside their academic specialization: a Ph.D. in American history employed by the United States Information Agency, a D.M.A. who owns and operates a used-book store, an M.F.A. in creative writing employed as a loan officer in a metropolitan bank, or an M.A. in biology serving as a legislative lobbyist. For most of these people, a new career was not just a matter of luck, and it didn't just happen overnight. Breaking away from traditional types of employment and conventional work settings is not easy for most Ph.D.'s and M.A.'s, nor can it be accomplished without a considerable amount of introspection and effort.

One of the first concerns is when to begin exploring other types of employment. As with any job search, there is no one moment when an individual comes to a full realization that the time is right. Exploring career options usually develops as the result of dissatisfaction or disappointment with the progress of a primary job search.

You may feel no need to expand your options if you were invited to interview for positions in your field and if you know that you were under serious consideration as a finalist in the selection process. If you have been a "runner-up" you can be reasonably sure that you are a viable candidate and that another job search in a new hiring season will afford a good chance of additional opportunities. Although you may need to find a temporary job to tide you over until you can secure the employment of your choice, persistence will probably be rewarded. On the other hand, if you did not receive serious consideration from any of your applications, you will need to evaluate your approach to your primary job search to determine if you can improve your strategies, techniques, and marketability. If you come to the conclusion that you have done all that you can do to promote your candidacy for available positions, a realistic assessment of your commitment and your goals may lead you to consider seriously the prospect of seeking optional employment.

Do not rush to adopt a new career plan. Exploring your options will involve some effort and a bit of research, but taking the time to evaluate your options can help you to avoid the disappointment, frustration, or unhappy underemployment that may accompany abrupt and unplanned career changes. It is always advisable to begin by identifying qualifications you currently possess rather than assuming that you need to acquire another degree which will make you more marketable. If you should decide that you want to prepare for another profession, retraining will undoubtedly be necessary. A new career as an attorney, engineer, librarian, counselor, or administrator may well require a specific degree program. Certainly, retraining is a valid route to a new career, but it should not be used as a substitute for career decisions or as a delaying tactic. Adding another degree is not necessarily the answer to your problem. For many people, a course or two may be all that is required to enhance qualifications for any number of jobs. For example, a beginning computer class can familiarize you with terms and allow you to understand the basic operating procedures of information systems. An introductory course in accounting will help you to master the vocabulary of business operations and acquaint you with routine business reports. Even one course in public speaking can increase your confidence and your ability to communicate effectively.

COMMON TRAPS TO AVOID

For many career changers it may be financially necessary to take the first job available, whether it's waiting tables, doing clerical work, tending bar, or driving a cab, but it is not necessary to settle into nonrelated or unsatisfying employment as a way of life. These jobs can be temporarily beneficial, but you must resist the traps that can keep you from pursuing your options for more appropriate and rewarding careers.

INERTIA

If you are supporting yourself, meeting your financial obligations, and not dreading every minute of your working day, the motivation to continue your professional job search or to explore career options can be diminished. It is easy to become complacent once the initial urgency of finding employment is alleviated.

LETTING YOUR JOB DEFINE YOU

Whether you are a cab driver or a college professor, your job does not define you. If you have a doctorate in English, for example, but have become a cab driver out of economic necessity, you may describe yourself in one of two ways: "I am a cab driver with a Ph.D." or "I am a scholar driving a cab." Either one may be correct, but the perception is markedly different. Defining yourself by your oc-cupation can allow you to fall victim to the cab-driver syndrome and discourage you from expanding your options.

SOUR GRAPES

If your primary job search has not been successful, it is natural to feel disappoint-ment, but indulging in self-pity or blaming the world for your predicament is counterproductive. Bitterness or hostility toward a career that did not develop the way you had anticipated, combined with the fear of being rejected or turned down again, can influence you to stay where you are as a protection from further disappointments or letdowns.

LACK OF SUPPORT

Your new colleagues and current employer may inhibit your career exploration because they do not understand what it is that you want to do or because they may want to keep you in the job you now hold. It is even possible for an em-ployer to intimidate you from pursuing other options. You should also be prepared for the possibility that support and encouragement from peers or your mentor will be noticeably lacking. It is not unheard of for a mentor to abandon a student who has not found a suitable job or to be less than supportive of a former student's decision to seek apparently unrelated employment.

FORMING REALISTIC EXPECTATIONS

Accepting the possibility that you may not find the kind of employment you en-visioned when you entered graduate school, and recognizing the dangers of be-coming trapped in jobs that do not allow full exercise of your qualifications and abilities, it is only natural for you to want immediate and concrete advice about other employment possibilities. If you are like most people, you have one thought in mind—"tell me where to go, tell me what to do!" Pinpointing specific jobs would be a quick solution; unfortunately, it is not that easy. No book, no work-shop, no placement counselor can prescribe a job for you, nor is such an expec-tation realistic. You are the only one who can make a career decision that will be right for you, but you may not yet have a clear picture of what it is that you need or want. You are beginning the process of finding out what others have done and what you can now begin to do.

SKILLS IDENTIFICATION

Once you decide to explore jobs other than those traditionally associated with your academic degree or specialization, you can begin to identify skills that can transfer to other types of employment. Identification of transferable skills will help you to determine the range of jobs for which you can apply and can be a major factor in the success of your applications. For example, if you think of yourself as a teacher, you should also be able to see yourself as a trainer. If you describe yourself as a teacher it is probably because you enjoy working with people and value the opportunity to share information with others, to lead them toward a preestablished objective, and to influence their thinking and their behavior. There may not be a single corporation or organization outside academe looking for someone to teach the courses you are prepared to offer, whether in medieval literature, baroque performance practices, or 19th-century rhetorical criticism. But there are many opportunities for people who can train others to communicate effectively, to interact positively, to organize their time productively, or to use equipment to enhance their message. If you describe yourself as primarily a researcher or analyst, the same basic skills that you exercised in scholarly pursuits can be applied to other areas. While your research orientation as a scholar may have been theoretical, the techniques and processes you have mastered can be transferred to applied research in another setting.

Most people agree that among the highly prized skills of advanced-degree job seekers is the ability to define problems, research a topic, analyze the findings, and present them concisely and coherently, either orally or in writing. Any graduate student has developed and exercised these skills in preparing for comprehensive exams and in writing papers, a thesis, or a dissertation, but with the emphasis on the final product the component skills are often overlooked. Most people who have completed an advanced degree are reasonably proficient in using these skills within their discipline, but few are adept at using these same skills to analyze themselves. There is often a shortsightedness or lack of recognition of transferability of previous successes to future endeavors. Presented with a rather typical list of skills valued by all employers, many academics ignore the most obvious connection between these words and their own accomplishments:

- develop
- supervise
- coordinate
- motivate
- evaluate
- manage
- market

- promote
- train
- analyze
- communicate
- implement
- initiate

By relating these words to your experience as a scholar or teacher you will be able to transfer them to employment in any setting. For example, you may not have thought of yourself as a supervisor but if you have taught you have developed objectives for each class session, organized materials, assigned and motivated students to perform specific tasks, and evaluated their efforts. If you were successful as a teacher, you were also able to market your ideas and to promote a product—your discipline. After you see the connection between these skills and your achievements you can effectively apply them to other types of activities or occupations.

In your effort to restructure your thinking to make it more compatible with what you imagine an employer wants to see or to hear about, it is very easy to ignore the obvious. Without the ability to demonstrate the application of these skills within your own field and within your own experiences, you will find it very difficult to convince an employer—or yourself—that the requisite skills are a part of your qualifications.

If you find it difficult to identify your skills and match them with career interests, vocational testing can be a useful tool. But you must remember that testing is only an indicator; it will not pinpoint a job for you. At best, it can suggest possible fields of interest for further exploration. Vocational counselors can offer suggestions, but they can only assist you with the analysis of your skills and interests—they cannot do your job for you. Regardless of what anyone tells you, you are the one who can and must take the responsibility for identifying and assessing your marketable skills.

DETERMINING PRIORITIES

In order to focus your job search and to get a clear idea of the types of employment options available, you need to identify priorities for a career that will offer rewards and satisfactions, such as:

- salary
- location
- status
- challenge
- upward mobility
- prestige of employer
- job security
- fringe benefits
- power
- work setting

- flexibility of working hours
- autonomy
- working relationships with colleagues
- variety
- leadership
- supervision
- opportunity to exercise creativity
- intellectual stimulation
- public contact

No one job will offer all these features, and not all of them will be of real importance or interest to you, but by analyzing these factors you can identify the employment sectors which can offer the kind of job that will meet your needs. Suppose you want to find a job that allows you to work with the public and that offers a high degree of challenge. Suppose further that your priorities also include an opportunity to exercise creativity and some degree of variety in daily activities. Using only these factors as your criteria, it would appear that you could find satisfaction as a sales representative for IBM or as a counselor in a locally funded substance-abuse clinic.

Obviously the picture changes dramatically with the addition of just one other factor—salary—and other relevant factors would widen the gap still further. You have to put as many factors together as you can reasonably assess in order to come up with a set of priorities that might be predictive of success or job satisfaction.

ADS, AGENCIES, AND NETWORKS

After analyzing your skills and determining your priorities, the next step is to identify potential employers who will recognize your skills as a marketable commodity. Your first impulse may be to look for listings of available jobs. The classified ad section of your daily newspaper is the easiest and most obvious starting point to get an idea of the types of positions available in your community; professional journals and trade publications can be consulted for announcements of openings in a wider geographic range. While published ads should never be overlooked, some people estimate that fewer than ten percent of the jobs available at any given time are advertised in print, and that most management or professional jobs are seldom advertised. It is also estimated that another ten percent of the jobs are listed with employment agencies. Private or commercial employment agencies vary in quality and are only as good as the people who staff them. Be cautious of agencies which want you to pay for résumé preparation or attend training programs at considerable cost. Compare fees and services—shop around for a good agency just as you would shop around for the best buy on a car. Don't pay for more than you need.

DEVELOPING A NEW NETWORK

If newspaper ads and employment agencies are useful in uncovering information about twenty percent of the available jobs, how do the other eighty percent get filled? Usually they are filled on the basis of personal contacts. Just as networks are important in academic and professional circles, they also can be instrumental in helping you find a position in any sector. Once you have determined your job objective, the next step is to begin meeting people who can help you—not necessarily those who can offer you a job, but people familiar with the occupation and people who know insiders in the kind of organization in which you are interested. Use the same techniques to build a network as you did in your primary job search. Don't keep your job search a secret; let everyone know that you are job hunting. If they can't help you, perhaps they know someone who can. Through this type of referral you can gradually build up a productive network which may include other people who are in the same process as you or who have successfully been through the system, found a job, and can now give you some very helpful advice.

ADAPTING JOB-SEARCH STRATEGIES

All of the tactics, techniques, and strategies you learned to use in your academic and professional job search need not be abandoned but adapted to your present job search. Any job search involves identifying potential employers and making initial contacts, developing appropriate documents, preparing for interviews, evaluating your performance, and following up with employers. An important part of marketing yourself involves locating, analyzing, and synthesizing information about the organization or firm which can offer employment. Those job seekers who take the time to learn something about the company or organization, its products or services, its reputation, its financial condition, and its long-range objectives are far more likely to succeed than those who depend upon inspiration and luck. Important as this type of information can be, you must never lose sight of the fact that you are not going to be hired for how much you know about the company or organization but for what you can contribute to it. Employers will be looking for evidence of your skills and abilities and for personal characteristics consistent with the values, philosophy, and objectives of the company and its current employees. Company literature available in college placement offices and campus libraries or trade association magazines can be consulted for detailed information.

VITA OUT, RÉSUMÉ IN

In order to convince employers of your commitment to the type of job for which you are now applying, it is critical for you to modify and alter the materials you present to prospective employers. The vita you prepared for academic positions will not be appropriate for jobs outside the academic community. When educational background is not a primary requisite for the position, a résumé allows you to present your qualifications in terms that will be meaningful to potential employers. Transforming an academic vita into a résumé is not just a matter of rearranging categories; relevant items must be retained, different items must often be incorporated, and irrelevant items must be deleted. Evaluation of previous experiences must be undertaken in order to focus the résumé on your current job objective. A résumé is not an all-purpose document; if you are considering a variety of positions it may be to your advantage to prepare more than one to emphasize different aspects of your background and experience. A one-page résumé is preferred and, of course, must be visually pleasing, accurate and current, and error-free. The following samples illustrate the transformation of an academic vita and a professional résumé into résumés which could be used for other employment options.

After deciding to seek employment outside the academic community, Christopher Asche has designed a résumé that can be used for a variety of positions. To give potential employers an overview of his achievements and skills, Christopher has created two complementary categories: Accomplishments and Competencies. The summary of activities and previous responsibilities demonstrates leadership capabilities and knowledge and experience of various sectors of the academic community as well as other interests. Items for these categories were selected from three sections of his vita (Teaching and Research Experience, Academic Training, and Conference Presentation) and from two sections of his new résumé (Part-Time and Summer Employment and Personal Interests). The statement of each accomplishment begins with a strong, active word. Complete sentences are not necessary; short phrases are easy to scan and hold the reader's interest. The Competencies section reinforces strengths and interests illustrated in the Accomplishments category. The list of words and phrases effectively summarizes skills and abilities without forcing the reader to abstract this information.

Because the responsibilities of Christopher's teaching and research experience have been outlined in the Accomplishments section, the Professional Experience category simply lists the title, location, and dates of his employment. Since the focus of this résumé is for a position that is not defined as teaching or research, the title of this section has been changed to Professional Experience.

Because Christopher's degrees and academic discipline are not primary qualifications or prerequisites for the type of position he is currently seeking, the Academic Training category presents basic information without elaboration. The study in England has been deleted from this category and presented in the Accomplishments section, and the specific information about comprehensive examination areas and dissertation topic has been deleted.

The Awards and Distinctions category has been retained because employers are always interested in superior performance and recognition. The only modification in this category has been to include the bachelor's degree honors.

Professional Memberships listed on the vita are not included on the résumé because they are all oriented toward a specific academic discipline. In order to keep the résumé to a one-page presentation, Christopher has chosen to replace the memberships category with other information which has greater relevance to a nonacademic employer.

The Part-Time and Summer Employment category not only illustrates that Christopher has had outside work experience but also indicates an ability to interact with people of varying academic and social backgrounds.

The Conference Presentation category does not appear on the résumé, but the information has been presented in general terms under the Accomplishments section. A Personal Interests category has been substituted because the range of interests can demonstrate a broad background and a variety of experiences which can be used in conversation with various individuals and groups.

Because Christopher's dossier is academically oriented, he has chosen to indicate that references relevant to this job search will be provided upon request.

Janine Swenson's original résumé was designed for a professional library position. As an outgrowth of her background in computer applications to library systems, Janine has decided to pursue a position with a company producing computer systems for libraries and information centers. Although she has been able to retain the basic format of her original résumé, her revised résumé has a completely different focus and emphasizes skills and background related to her current objective.

Two new categories have been created: Areas of Knowledge and Course Highlights. The first category allows Janine to display her familiarity with computer systems and her ability to implement various programs. The courses listed in the second category have been carefully selected to emphasize her background in computers, her knowledge of management techniques, and her oral communication skills.

Because Janine is not seeking a library position, she has changed the category heading from Library Experience to Experience. For each position listed, Janine has identified the employer and the location followed by the title of her position. Instead of describing each position separately, she has summarized the responsibilities of all three positions in order to eliminate items specifically related to library work and to concentrate on those areas of responsibility which more clearly relate to her new objective. Short phrases rather than lengthy descriptions make it easy for the reader to scan the résumé and to identify skills, background, and experience almost at a glance.

The Community Activities section of Janine's résumé has been retained because it can help to demonstrate to potential employers that she is an active person with varied interests. Because it is not directly applicable to her objective, Janine has moved her volunteer work with a church library from the Experience section to the Community Activities category.

Because Janine's educational background will be of interest to her potential employers but is not a primary qualification for the type of position she is seek-

SAMPLE VITA

CHRISTOPHER J. ASCHE

ADDRESSES

Home: 421 Walnut
Tempe, Arizona 85281
(602) 248-3001

Office: 3121 Communications Center
Arizona State University
Tempe, Arizona 85281
(602) 248-1782

ACADEMIC TRAINING

Hiram College Hiram, Ohio	1974–1978	B.A. cum laude	English
The Ohio State University Columbus, Ohio	1978–1979	M.A.	English
Arizona State University Tempe, Arizona	1979–	Ph.D.	English
Cambridge University Cambridge, England	1981–1982		Elizabethan/Jacobean Drama

Comprehensive areas include: Renaissance Literature, 18th Century British Literature, Expository Writing.

Dissertation Title: Aesthetic Distance in the Early Comedies of Ben Jonson.

TEACHING AND RESEARCH EXPERIENCE

Teaching Assistant, Communications Program, Arizona State University, 1979–1981 Complete responsibility for instruction and grading of a two-semester freshman course stressing development of oral and written communication skills.

Research Assistant, Arizona State University, 1982–1983 Assisted Professors Gould and Perry in a review of the literature for a federally funded grant to implement a program in expository writing.

AWARDS AND DISTINCTIONS

Dean's List, Hiram College, 1974–1978
Homeier Senior Scholarship, Hiram College, 1977–1978
Who's Who in American Colleges, 1978
Representative, Arizona State University Student Senate, 1980–1981
The Robert Fay Literary Fellowship, 1981–1982
Student member, Departmental Advisory Committee, Arizona State University, 1979–present

PROFESSIONAL MEMBERSHIPS

Modern Language Association
Southwest Modern Language Association
Conference on College Composition and Communication

CONFERENCE PRESENTATION

"Myth and Fabliau: Sources for Jonson's *Volpone*," at the Southwest Modern Language Association Conference, Phoenix, Arizona, March, 1983

Complete dossier available from the Placement Center, McLean Hall, Arizona State University, Tempe, Arizona 85281   (602) 248-2022

RÉSUMÉ

CHRISTOPHER J. ASCHE
421 Walnut
Tempe, Arizona 85281
(602) 248-3001 (home)
(602) 248-1782 (office)

ACCOMPLISHMENTS

Planned and conducted class activities and evaluated development of communication skills for 206 individuals

Provided individual consultation and assistance for freshman and sophomore students

Represented peers in committee assignments and student government

Participated in $100,000 federally funded project to implement new program and reviewed more than 800 documents to compile summary report for senior researcher

Traveled and studied in England to conduct preliminary research for final project

Prepared and delivered address for regional professional conference

Founded and coordinated activities for Skydiving Club currently comprising 60 members

COMPETENCIES

Writing	Research	Supervision
Speaking	Program Development	Public Relations

PROFESSIONAL EXPERIENCE

Teaching Assistant, Communications Program, Arizona State University, Tempe, Arizona, 1978–1981

Research Assistant, Expository Writing, Arizona State University, Tempe, Arizona, 1982–1983

ACADEMIC TRAINING

Hiram College, Hiram, Ohio, 1974–1978   B.A.   English
The Ohio State University, Columbus, Ohio, 1978–1979   M.A.   English
Arizona State University, Tempe, Arizona, 1979–present   Ph.D.   English

AWARDS AND DISTINCTIONS

Dean's List, Hiram College, 1974–1978
Homeier Senior Scholarship, Hiram College, 1977–1978
Who's Who in American Colleges, 1978
Representative, Arizona State University Student Senate, 1980–1981
The Robert Fay Literary Fellowship, 1981–1982
Student member, Departmental Advisory Committee, Arizona State University, 1979–present

PART-TIME AND SUMMER EMPLOYMENT

Sales clerk, Esquire Menswear, Columbus, Ohio, 1978–1979
Construction worker, County Highway Department, Chagrin Falls, Ohio, summers 1974–1977
Cashier, College Bookstore, Hiram, Ohio, 1976–1978

PERSONAL INTERESTS

Skydiving, spectator sports, classical music, carpentry

REFERENCES AVAILABLE UPON REQUEST

RÉSUMÉ

JANINE M. SWENSON

ADDRESS	6200 28th Avenue North Minneapolis, Minnesota 55427 (612) 533-5018
OBJECTIVE	Professional public library position. Special interest in reference, computer applications, and materials selection.
EDUCATION	M.L.S., University of Minnesota, Minneapolis, Minnesota, 1983 B.A., Concordia College, Moorhead, Minnesota, 1982 Majors: German and Sociology A.A., Golden Valley Lutheran College, Golden Valley, Minnesota, 1980 Major: Liberal Arts
LIBRARY EXPERIENCE	Library Practicum, St. Paul Public Library, St. Paul, Minnesota March–June, 1983. Practicum included reference and reader's advisory services, materials selection and collection evaluation, program planning and publicity, and outreach program at Ramsay County Jail. Field Experience, Golden Valley Branch, Hennepin County Libraries, Golden Valley, Minnesota, January–March, 1983. Observation of branch library operations and administration, with emphasis on library and media maintenance, budgetary planning, and computer applications in circulation. Circulation Clerk, Concordia College Library, Moorhead, Minnesota, 1980–82. Hired as page, promoted to circulation clerk after three months. Duties included charging out materials, serving at guard desk and various clerical tasks. Volunteer Librarian, Elim Lutheran Church, Robbinsdale, Minnesota, Summer, 1982. Responsible for weeding of collection and selection of new materials for children and young adults. Assisted with revising circulation procedures and promotion of library use.
HONORS AND AWARDS	Scholarship award, University of Minnesota School of Library Science Dean's list, 1978–82, B.A. awarded with honors Phi Theta Kappa honorary society
COMMUNITY ACTIVITIES	Member, Hennepin County Oral History Society Softball Coach, Crystal Park and Recreation Program Member, Fundraising Committee, American Swedish Institute
REFERENCES	Placement file available from School of Library Science B16 Walter Library University of Minnesota Minneapolis, Minnesota 55455

REVISED RÉSUMÉ

JANINE M. SWENSON

ADDRESS	6200 28th Avenue North Minneapolis, Minnesota 55427 (612) 533-5018

AREAS OF KNOWLEDGE	Computer Languages COBOL, PASCAL, FORTRAN Hardware & Software Evaluation Feasibility Studies	Records Maintenance Computer Conversion Information Services

COURSE
HIGHLIGHTS
	Programming Language
	   Concepts
	Computer Packages for
	   Statistical Analysis
	Social Simulations and
	   Educational Computing
		Principles of Management
		Introduction to Systems Software
		Management of Libraries and
		   Information Centers
		Public Speaking

EXPERIENCE	St. Paul Public Library, St. Paul, Minnesota, 1983
	   Position: Graduate Practicum Student
	Golden Valley Branch, Hennepin County Libraries, Golden
	   Valley, Minnesota, 1983
	   Position: Graduate Internship
	Concordia College Library, Moorhead, Minnesota, 1980–82
	   Position: Circulation Clerk
	
	   Responsibilities in these positions included:
	      computer applications
	      program planning and publicity
	      budget preparation
	      outreach programming
	      public services
	      evaluation and maintenance studies

COMMUNITY ACTIVITIES	Volunteer Librarian, Elim Lutheran Church, Robbinsdale, Minnesota Member, Hennepin County Oral History Society Softball Coach, Crystal Park and Recreation Program Member, Fundraising Committee, American Swedish Institute

EDUCATION	University of Minnesota, Minneapolis, Minnesota
	   Master's Degree in Library Science, 1983
	Concordia College, Moorhead, Minnesota
	   Bachelor of Arts Degree in German and Sociology
	Golden Valley Lutheran College, Golden Valley, Minnesota
	   Associate of Arts Degree in Liberal Arts

HONORS AND AWARDS	Scholarship award, University of Minnesota School of Library Science Dean's list, 1978–82, B.A. awarded with honors Phi Theta Kappa honorary society

REFERENCES	Upon request

ing, she has moved the Education section of her résumé to a less prominent position near the bottom of the page. She has retained the reverse chronology in presenting her education, but she has deemphasized the degrees by placing them after the name of the institution attended and, because business employers may not be familiar with the abbreviation M.L.S., Janine has spelled out the degrees.

The Honors & Awards category has been retained because employers in the business sector are also interested in academic achievement and distinction.

Because a business employer is less likely to expect to receive a dossier, Janine has changed her References category to state that references are available upon request. She may simply provide names and telephone numbers of people familiar with her work rather than submitting written recommendations.

DON'T LOOK BACK

Adapting your résumé is comparatively simple, but perhaps the most important modification concerns your attitude and perception of yourself and your abilities. In the academic world your degree is a primary qualification and, in most cases, an absolute requirement for a specific position. In other spheres the degree is no longer paramount and is of far less importance than your potential. You cannot depend on your degree as a selling point, but it should never be considered a liability. While there is no need to hide—or apologize for—a doctorate, do not make it an issue if it is not relevant to your qualifications for the position. Introducing yourself as "Dr. John Smith" can give the impression that you are arrogant, naive, or just a misplaced academic. Leave your title in the elevator or check it at the door. It is important for you to concentrate on—and to help the employer focus on—the skills and abilities you have acquired through your graduate study rather than on the string of letters you are entitled to append to your signature.

Most employers do not consciously reject applicants simply because they hold an advanced degree, but if you place undue emphasis on your academic achievements they may wonder why you are applying for a job with their organization. In order to market yourself effectively you have to be able to convince employers that you are a viable candidate worthy of their consideration. Ask yourself the following questions. Can I convince the employer:

- that I can contribute to the organization?
- that I am not overqualified for the position?
- that my degree (or academic training) will not create a barrier between me and my coworkers or supervisors?
- that I can work under stress, pressure, and deadlines?
- that I do not object to overtime, travel, or rotating shifts?

- that I have a genuine interest in this line of work?
- that I do not see myself as a failed academic?

The ability to convince a potential employer to hire you will, of course, depend upon your ability to convince yourself that you are capable and that you are willing to commit your energies to this type of career. You have to believe that the decision to expand your options represents a legitimate career choice, that it does not reflect negatively on your educational background, and that you are not simply settling for second best. If you have been able to expand your options through a careful and calculated exploration of career paths, you need not apologize to yourself or to anyone else. You can feel justifiably proud of your accomplishment, and enjoy both the personal and professional rewards of your new employment.

Appendixes

Accrediting Associations

Middle States Association of Colleges and Schools
3624 Market Street, Philadelphia, Pennsylvania 19104

States include: Delaware, Maryland, New Jersey, New York, and Pennsylvania. Also, the District of Columbia, Puerto Rico, and the Virgin Islands.

New England Association of Schools and Colleges
131 Middlesex Turnpike, Burlington, Massachusetts 01803

States include: Connecticut, Maine, Massachusetts, New Hampshire, Rhode Island, and Vermont.

North Central Association of Colleges and Schools
159 Dearborn Street, Chicago, Illinois 60601

States include: Arizona, Arkansas, Colorado, Illinois, Indiana, Iowa, Kansas, Michigan, Minnesota, Missouri, Nebraska, New Mexico, North Dakota, Ohio, Oklahoma, South Dakota, West Virginia, Wisconsin, and Wyoming.

Northwest Association of Schools and Colleges
3700-B University Way, NE, Seattle, Washington 98105

States include: Alaska, Idaho, Montana, Nevada, Oregon, Utah, and Washington.

Southern Association of Colleges and Schools
795 Peachtree Street, NE, Atlanta, Georgia 30365

States include: Alabama, Florida, Georgia, Kentucky, Louisiana, Mississippi, North Carolina, South Carolina, Tennessee, Texas, and Virginia.

Western Association of Schools and Colleges
Mills College, Box 9990, Oakland, California 94613

States include: California and Hawaii. Also, American Samoa, Guam, and the Trust Territory of the Pacific.

Selected List of Academic and Professional Associations

ARTS

Art & Art History

American Art Therapy Association
5999 Stevenson Avenue
Alexandria, Virginia 22304

College Art Association of America
149 Madison Avenue
New York, New York 10016

National Art Education Association
1916 Association Drive
Reston, Virginia 22091

National Council on Education for
the Ceramic Arts
P.O. Box 1677
Bandon, Oregon 97411

Arts Management & Museums

American Association of Museums
1055 Thomas Jefferson Street, NW
Washington, D.C. 20007

American Institute for Conservation of
Historic and Artistic Works
3545 Williamsburg Lane
Washington, D.C. 20008

Association of College, University and
Community Arts Administrators
6225 University Avenue
Madison, Wisconsin 53705

International Society of Performing
Arts Administrators
Performing Arts Center
University of Texas
Austin, Texas 78712

Music

American Association for Music
Therapy
Suite 1601, 211 East 43rd Street
New York, New York 10017

American Choral Directors Association
Box 6310
Lawton, Oklahoma 73506

American Musicological Society
Room 205, 201 South 34th Street
Philadelphia, Pennsylvania 19104

American Society of University
Composers
Room 300, 250 West 54th Street
New York, New York 10019

American String Teachers Association
  Georgia University Station
  Box 2066
  Athens, Georgia 30602

College Band Directors National
Association
  School of Music
  Baylor University
  Waco, Texas 76798

College Music Society
  University of Colorado
  Box 44
  Boulder, Colorado 80309

International Association of Organ
Teachers USA
  7938 Bertram Avenue
  Hammond, Indiana 46324

International Piano Guild
  808 Rio Grande Street, Box 1807
  Austin, Texas 78767

Music Educators National Conference
  1902 Association Drive
  Reston, Virginia 22091

Music Teachers National Association
  2113 Carew Tower
  Cincinnati, Ohio 45202

National Association for Music Therapy
  Suite 800
  1001 Connecticut Avenue, NW
  Washington, D.C. 20036

National Association of College Wind
and Percussion Instructors
  Division of Fine Arts
  Northeast Missouri State University
  Kirksville, Missouri 63501

National Association of Jazz Educators
  Box 724
  Manhattan, Kansas 66502

National Association of Teachers
of Singing
  Suite 778, 35 West 4th Street
  New York, New York 10003

National Band Association
  Box 3228
  Augusta, Georgia 30904

National Guild of Community Schools
of the Arts
  Box 583, West Englewood Station
  Teaneck, New Jersey 07666

Percussive Arts Society
  214 West Main Street
  Urbana, Illinois 61801

Society for Ethnomusicology
  P.O. Box 2984
  Ann Arbor, Michigan 48106

Theater & Dance

American Dance Therapy Association
  Suite 108, 2000 Century Plaza
  Columbia, Maryland 21044

American Society for Theatre Research
  Department of English
  Queens College
  Flushing, New York 11367

American Theatre Association
  6th Floor
  1010 Wisconsin Avenue, NW
  Washington, D.C. 20007

Congress on Research in Dance
  Department of Dance Education
  New York University
  35 West 4th Street
  New York, New York 10003

National Dance Association
  1900 Association Drive
  Reston, Virginia 22091

Speech Communication Association
5105 Backlick Road
Annandale, Virginia 22003

HUMANITIES

Languages & Literature

American Association for Applied
Linguistics
3520 Prospect Street, NW
Washington, D.C. 20007

American Association of Teachers
of Arabic
University of Chicago
1155 East 58th Street
Chicago, Illinois 60637

American Association of Teachers
of French
57 East Armory
Champaign, Illinois 61820

American Association of Teachers
of German
523 Building, Suite 201, Route 38
Cherry Hill, New Jersey 08034

American Association of Teachers
of Italian
Italian Department
Indiana University
Bloomington, Indiana 47401

American Association of Teachers of
Slavic and East European Languages
Department of Russian
University of Arizona
Tucson, Arizona 87521

American Association of Teachers
of Spanish and Portuguese
University of Mississippi
University, Mississippi 38677

American Classical League
Miami University
Oxford, Ohio 45056

American Comparative Literature
Association
University of Michigan
Ann Arbor, Michigan 48109

American Council on the Teaching
of Foreign Languages, Inc.
579 Broadway
Hastings-on-Hudson,
New York 10706

American Philological Association
617 Hamilton Hall
Columbia University
New York, New York 10027

American Translators Association
109 Croton Avenue
Ossining, New York 10562

Associated Writing Programs
Old Dominion University
Norfolk, Virginia 23508

Chinese Language Teachers Association
Institute of Far Eastern Studies
Seton Hall University
South Orange, New Jersey 07070

College English Association
University of Houston
1 Main Street
Houston, Texas 77004

College Language Association
Atlanta University
Atlanta, Georgia 30314

Conference on College Composition
and Communication
111 Kenyon Road
Urbana, Illinois 61801

Linguistic Society of America
    3520 Prospect Street, NW
    Washington, D.C. 20007

Modern Language Association
of America
    62 Fifth Avenue
    New York, New York 10011

National Council of Teachers of English
    111 Kenyon Road
    Urbana, Illinois 61801

Teachers of English to Speakers
of Other Languages
    202 D.C. Transit Building
    Georgetown University
    Washington, D.C. 20057

Philosophy & Religion

American Academy of Religion
    Syracuse University
    Syracuse, New York 13210

American Philosophical Association
    University of Delaware
    31 Amstel Avenue
    Newark, Delaware 19711

American Society of Church History
    305 East Country Club Lane
    Wallingford, Pennsylvania 19086

Association for the Sociology
of Religion
    Washington and Jefferson College
    Washington, Pennsylvania 15301

Association of Professors and
Researchers in Religious Education
    Chicago Cluster of Theological
    Schools
    1100 East 55th Street
    Chicago, Illinois 60615

Council on the Study of Religion
    Wilfred Laurier University
    Waterloo, Ontario N2L 3C5
    Canada

MATHEMATICS, ENGINEERING, AND TECHNOLOGY

Computer & Information Science

American Association for Artificial
Intelligence
    445 Burgess Drive
    Menlo Park, California 94025

American Federation of Information
Processing Societies
    1899 Preston White Drive
    Reston, Virginia 22091

American Society for Information
Science
    1010 16th Street, NW
    Washington, D.C. 20036

Association for Computing Machinery
    11 West 42nd Street
    New York, New York 10036

Association for Educational Data
Systems
    1201 16th Street, NW
    Washington, D.C. 20036

International Council for Computers
in Education
    University of Oregon
    1787 Agate Street
    Eugene, Oregon 97403

Society for Applied Learning
Technology
    50 Culpeper Street
    Warrenton, Virginia 22186

Society for Information Management
Suite 600, 111 East Wacker Drive
Chicago, Illinois 60601

Engineering

American Institute of Chemical
Engineers
345 East 47th Street
New York, New York 10017

American Institute of Industrial
Engineers
25 Technology Park/Atlanta
Norcross, Georgia 30092

American Institute of Mining,
Metallurgical and Petroleum Engineers
345 East 47th Street
New York, New York 10017

American Society for Engineering
Education
Eleven Dupont Circle, NW, Suite 200
Washington, D.C. 20036

American Society of Agricultural
Engineers
2950 Niles Road
St. Joseph, Michigan 49085

American Society of Civil Engineers
345 East 47th Street
New York, New York 10017

American Society of Mechanical
Engineers
345 East 47th Street
New York, New York 10017

Association of Energy Engineers
Suite 340, 4025 Pleasantdale Road
Atlanta, Georgia 30340

Association of Engineering Geologists
Box 506
Short Hills, New Jersey 07078

Association of Environmental
Engineering Professors
Department of Civil Engineering
Villanova University
Villanova, Pennsylvania 19085

Institute of Environmental Sciences
940 East Northwest Highway
Mt. Prospect, Illinois 60056

Institute of Transportation Engineers
Suite 410, 525 School Street, SW
Washington, D.C. 20024

International Federation of
Professional and Technical Engineers
818 Roeder Road
Silver Spring, Maryland 20910

National Society of Professional
Engineers
2029 K Street, NW
Washington, D.C. 20006

Society of Automotive Engineers
400 Commonwealth Drive
Warrendale, Pennsylvania 15096

Mathematics

American Academy of Actuaries
Suite 515, 1835 K Street, NW
Washington, D.C. 20006

American Mathematical Society
Box 6248
Providence, Rhode Island 02940

American Statistical Association
Suite 640, 806 15th Street, NW
Washington, D.C. 20005

Institute of Mathematical Statistics
Department of Statistics
University of California, Berkeley
Berkeley, California 94720

Mathematical Association of America
1529 18th Street, NW
Washington, D.C. 20036

National Council of Teachers
of Mathematics
1906 Association Drive
Reston, Virginia 22091

Society for Industrial and Applied
Mathematics
1405 Architects Building
117 South 17th Street
Philadelphia, Pennsylvania 19103

SCIENCES

Biological Sciences

American Association for the
Advancement of Science
1515 Massachusetts Avenue, NW
Washington, D.C. 20005

American Association of Anatomists
Department of Anatomy
Medical College of Virginia
Richmond, Virginia 23298

American Institute of Biological
Sciences
1401 Wilson Boulevard
Arlington, Virginia 22209

The American Society for Cell Biology
9650 Rockville Pike
Bethesda, Maryland 20814

American Society for Microbiology
1913 I Street, NW
Washington, D.C. 20006

American Society of Naturalists
Department of Biology
University of Rochester
Rochester, New York 14627

Botanical Society of America
School of Biological Sciences
University of Kentucky
Lexington, Kentucky 40506

Federation of American Societies
for Experimental Biology
9650 Rockville Pike
Bethesda, Maryland 20814

Health & Behavioral Sciences

American College Health Association
Suite 208, 152 Rollins Avenue
Rockville, Maryland 20852

American College of Hospital
Administrators
840 North Lake Shore Drive
Chicago, Illinois 60611

American Dietetic Association
430 North Michigan Avenue
Chicago, Illinois 60611

American Nurses Association
2420 Pershing Road
Kansas City, Missouri 64108

American Occupational Therapy
Association
Suite 300, 1338 Piccard Drive
Rockville, Maryland 20850

American Physical Therapy Association
1111 North Fairfax Street
Alexandria, Virginia 22314

American Psychological Association
1200 17th Street, NW
Washington, D.C. 20036

American Public Health Association
1015 15th Street, NW
Washington, D.C. 20005

American Society of Allied Health Professions
Suite 300, One Dupont Circle, NW
Washington, D.C. 20036

American Speech and Hearing Association
10801 Rockville Pike
Rockville, Maryland 20852

Association for Hospital Medical Education
Suite 700
1101 Connecticut Avenue, NW
Washington, D.C. 20036

Association of Mental Health Administrators
425 13th Street, NW
Washington, D.C. 20004

National Association of Physical Therapists
P.O. Box 367
West Covine, California 91793

National League for Nursing
10 Columbus Circle
New York, New York 10019

Society for Nutrition Education
1736 Franklin Street
Oakland, California 94612

Society for Public Health Education
Suite 535, 703 Market Street
San Francisco, California 94103

Natural Resources

American Association of Teacher Educators in Agriculture
Department of Agricultural Education
102 Morrill Hall
North Dakota State University
Fargo, North Dakota 58105

American Fisheries Society
5410 Grosvenor Lane
Bethesda, Maryland 20814

American Forestry Association
1319 18th Street, NW
Washington, D.C. 20036

American Genetic Association
818 18th Street, NW
Washington, D.C. 20006

American Society of Agronomy
677 South Segoe Road
Madison, Wisconsin 53711

American Society of Animal Science
309 West Clark Street
Champaign, Illinois 61820

American Veterinary Medical Association
930 North Meachum Road
Schaumburg, Illinois 60196

Council for Agricultural Science and Technology
250 Memorial Union
Ames, Iowa 50011

National Association of Colleges and Teachers of Agriculture
University of Illinois
608 West Vermont
Urbana, Illinois 61801

National Association of Environmental Professionals
815 Second Avenue
New York, New York 10017

Society of American Foresters
5400 Grosvenor Lane
Bethesda, Maryland 20814

Soil Conservation Society of America
7515 Northeast Ankeny Road
Ankeny, Iowa 50021

Physical Sciences

American Association for Clinical
Chemistry
    1725 K Street, NW
    Washington, D.C. 20006

American Association of Physics
Teachers
    Graduate Physics Building
    State University of New York
    at Stony Brook
    Stony Brook, New York 11794

American Astronomical Society
    1816 Jefferson Place, NW
    Washington, D.C. 20036

American Chemical Society
    1155 16th Street, NW
    Washington, D.C. 20036

American Geological Institute
    Suite 1501, 25 West 39th Street
    New York, New York 10018

American Institute of Chemists
    7315 Wisconsin Avenue
    Bethesda, Maryland 20814

American Institute of Physics
    335 East 45th Street
    New York, New York 10017

Geological Society of America
    3300 Penrose Place, Box 9140
    Boulder, Colorado 80301

National Association of Geology
Teachers
    Department of Environmental
        Resources
    Bureau of Topographical and
        Geological Survey
    Harrisburg, Pennsylvania 17120

SOCIAL SCIENCES

Area Studies

African Studies Association
    255 Kinsey Hall
    University of California, Los Angeles
    Los Angeles, California 90024

American Association for Chinese
Studies
    Sun Yat Sen Hall
    St. John's University
    Jamaica, New York 11439

American Association for the
Advancement of Slavic Studies
    Stanford University, Box A-0
    Stanford, California 94305

American Studies Association
    307 College Hall
    University of Pennsylvania
    Philadelphia, Pennsylvania 19104

Association for Asian Studies
    1 Lane Hall
    University of Michigan
    Ann Arbor, Michigan 48109

Association for the Study of
Afro-American Life and History
    1401 14th Street, NW
    Washington, D.C. 20005

International Studies Association
    Byrnes International Center
    Columbia, South Carolina 29208

Latin American Studies Association
    Institute of Latin American Studies
    University of Texas
    Austin, Texas 78712

Middle East Studies Association
of North America
   Department of Oriental Studies
   University of Arizona
   Tucson, Arizona 85721

Society for the Advancement
of Scandinavian Study
   Germanic Languages
   University of Illinois
   Urbana, Illinois 61801

Business/Economics

Academy of International Business
   World Trade Education Center
   Cleveland State University
   Cleveland, Ohio 44115

American Economic Association
   1313 21st Avenue South
   Nashville, Tennessee 37212

American Finance Association
   Graduate School of Business
   Administration
   New York University
   100 Trinity Place
   New York, New York 10006

American Management Associations
   135 West 50th Street
   New York, New York 10020

American Marketing Association
   Suite 200, 250 South Wacker Drive
   Chicago, Illinois 60606

American Society for Public
Administration
   1120 G Street, NW
   Washington, D.C. 20005

American Society for Training
and Development
   600 Maryland Avenue, SW
   Washington, D.C. 20024

Association for Evolutionary
Economics
   Department of Economics
   University of Nebraska
   Lincoln, Nebraska 68588

Econometric Society
   Department of Economics
   Northwestern University
   Evanston, Illinois 60201

Economic History Association
   c/o Eleutherian Mills Historical
   Library
   Greenville, Delaware 19807

Financial Management Association
   College of Business Administration
   University of South Florida
   Tampa, Florida 33620

National Business Education
Association
   1914 Association Drive
   Reston, Virginia 22091

Communications

American Society of Educators
   1511 Walnut Street
   Philadelphia, Pennsylvania 19102

Association for Educational
Communications and Technology
   1126 16th Street, NW
   Washington, D.C. 20036

Association for Education in
Journalism and Mass Communication
   College of Journalism
   University of South Carolina
   Columbia, South Carolina 29208

Association of Teachers of Technical
Writing
   Hinds Junior College
   Raymond, Mississippi 39154

Broadcast Education Association
1771 N Street, NW
Washington, D.C. 20036

Community College Journalism
Association
3600 North Garfield
Midland, Texas 79705

International Communication
Association
Suite 828, 12750 Merit Drive
Dallas, Texas 75251

National Association of Educational
Broadcasters
5807 Massachusetts Avenue, NW
Bethesda, Maryland 20816

Society for Technical Communication
Suite 506, 815 15th Street, NW
Washington, D.C. 20005

Speech Communication Association
5105 Backlick Road
Annandale, Virginia 22003

Education

American Association for Adult
and Continuing Education
Suite 230, 1201 16th Street, NW
Washington, D.C. 20036

American Association for Higher
Education
Suite 600, One Dupont Circle, NW
Washington, D.C. 20036

American Association of Colleges
for Teacher Education
Suite 610, One Dupont Circle, NW
Washington, D.C. 20036

American Association of Collegiate
Registrars and Admissions Officers
Suite 330, One Dupont Circle, NW
Washington, D.C. 20036

American Association of University
Professors
Suite 500, One Dupont Circle, NW
Washington, D.C. 20036

American College Personnel
Association
5999 Stevenson Avenue
Alexandria, Virginia 22304

American Educational Research
Association
1230 17th Street, NW
Washington, D.C. 20036

American Vocational Association, Inc.
2020 North 14th Street
Arlington, Virginia 22201

Association for Childhood Education
International
3615 Wisconsin Avenue, NW
Washington, D.C. 20016

Association for Educational
Communications and Technology
1126 16th Street, NW
Washington, D.C. 20036

Association for Supervision and
Curriculum Development
225 North Washington Street
Alexandria, Virginia 22314

Association of Teacher Educators
Suite ATE, 1900 Association Drive
Reston, Virginia 22091

International Reading Association
800 Barksdale Road, Box 8139
Newark, Delaware 19714

National Association for Women
Deans, Administrators and Counselors
1625 I Street, NW, 624-A
Washington, D.C. 20006

National Association of College
Admissions Counselors
   9933 Lawler Avenue, Suite 500
   Skokie, Illinois 60077

National Association of Student
Personnel Administrators
   160 Rightmere Hall
   1060 Carmack Road
   Columbus, Ohio 43210

History/Political Science/Geography

Academy of Political Science
   2852 Broadway
   New York, New York 10025

American Association for State
and Local History
   708 Berry Road
   Nashville, Tennessee 37204

American Geographical Society
   Suite 1501, 25 West 39th Street
   New York, New York 10018

American Historical Association
   400 A Street, SE
   Washington, D.C. 20003

American Political Science Association
   1527 New Hampshire Avenue, NW
   Washington, D.C. 20036

Association of American Geographers
   1710 16th Street, NW
   Washington, D.C. 20009

National Council for Geographic
Education
   Western Illinois University
   Macomb, Illinois 61455

Organization of American Historians
   Indiana University
   112 North Bryan Street
   Bloomington, Indiana 47401

Society for History Education
   California State University
   1240 Bellflower Boulevard
   Long Beach, California 90840

Society of American Archivists
   Suite 810, 330 South Wells Street
   Chicago, Illinois 60606

Human Services

Academy of Criminal Justice Sciences
   University of Nebraska
   1313 Farnam on the Mall
   Omaha, Nebraska 68182

American Association for Counseling
and Development
   5999 Stevenson Avenue
   Alexandria, Virginia 22304

American Association for Marriage
and Family Therapy
   Suite 407, 1717 K Street, NW
   Washington, D.C. 20006

American Correctional Association
   4321 Hartwick Road, Suite L-208
   College Park, Maryland 20740

American Mental Health Counselors
Association
   5999 Stevenson Avenue
   Alexandria, Virginia 22304

American Society of Criminology
   Ohio State University
   1314 Kinnera Road, Suite 214
   Columbus, Ohio 43212

Council on Social Work Education
   111 Eighth Avenue
   New York, New York 10011

National Association of Social Workers
   7981 Eastern Avenue
   Silver Spring, Maryland 20910

National Council on Family Relations
1219 University Avenue, SE
Minneapolis, Minnesota 55414

National Rehabilitation Association
633 South Washington Street
Alexandria, Virginia 22314

National Rehabilitation Counseling
Association
633 South Washington Street
Alexandria, Virginia 22314

Library

American Association of Law Libraries
53 West Jackson
Chicago, Illinois 60604

American Association of School
Librarians
50 East Huron Street
Chicago, Illinois 60611

American Library Association
50 East Huron Street
Chicago, Illinois 60611

American Society for Information
Science
1010 16th Street, NW
Washington, D.C. 20036

American Theological Library
Association
5600 South Woodlawn Avenue
Chicago, Illinois 60637

Art Libraries Society/North America
3775 Bear Creek Circle
Tucson, Arizona 85749

Association for Library and
Information Science Education
471 Park Lane
State College, Pennsylvania 16801

Association for Library Service
to Children
50 East Huron Street
Chicago, Illinois 60611

Association of College and Research
Libraries
50 East Huron Street
Chicago, Illinois 60611

Council of Planning Librarians
1313 East 60th Street
Chicago, Illinois 60637

Medical Library Association
919 North Michigan Avenue
Suite 3208
Chicago, Illinois 60611

Music Library Association
Box 487
Canton, Massachusetts 02021

Society of American Archivists
330 South Wells Street, Suite 810
Chicago, Illinois 60610

Special Libraries Association
235 Park Avenue South
New York, New York 10003

Theatre Library Association
111 Amsterdam Avenue
New York, New York 10023

Physical Education/Recreation/Sports

American Alliance for Health, Physical
Education, Recreation and Dance
1900 Association Drive
Reston, Virginia 22091

American Association for Leisure
and Recreation
1900 Association Drive
Reston, Virginia 22091

American Athletic Trainers Association
and Certification Board
  660 West Duarte Road
  Arcadia, California 91006

Association for the Advancement
of Health Education
  1900 Association Drive
  Reston, Virginia 22091

College Sports Information Directors
of America
  Campus Box 114
  Texas A&I University
  Kingsville, Texas 78363

National Association for Physical
Education in Higher Education
  Department of Physical Education
  Illinois State University
  Normal, Illinois 61761

National Association of Collegiate
Directors of Athletics
  1229 Smith Court
  Cleveland, Ohio 44116

National Athletic Trainers Association
  Box 1865
  Greenville, North Carolina 27834

National Recreation and Park
Association
  3101 Park Center Drive
  Alexandria, Virginia 22302

National Therapeutic Recreation
Society
  3101 Park Center Drive
  Alexandria, Virginia 22302

North American Society for the
Psychology of Sport and Physical
Activity
  University of Tennessee
  Knoxville, Tennessee 37996

Society of Park and Recreation
Educators
  3101 Park Center Drive
  Alexandria, Virginia 22302

Sociology/Anthropology/Archaeology

American Anthropological Association
  1703 New Hampshire Avenue, NW
  Washington, D.C. 20009

American Association of Physical
Anthropologists
  1703 New Hampshire Avenue, NW
  Washington, D.C. 20009

American Ethnological Society
  Department of Anthropology
  University of South Florida
  Tampa, Florida 33620

American Institute for Archaeological
Research
  Box 485
  Derry, New Hampshire 03038

American Society for Conservation
Archaeology
  22258 Covello Street
  Canoga Park, California 91304

American Society for Ethnohistory
  Department of Anthropology
  Texas Tech University
  Lubbock, Texas 79409

American Sociological Association
  1722 N Street, NW
  Washington, D.C. 20036

Archaeological Institute of America
  Box 1901, Kenmore Station
  Boston, Massachusetts 02215

Association for Field Archaeology
  Boston University
  745 Commonwealth Avenue
  Boston, Massachusetts 02215

Institute of Nautical Archaeology
  Drawer AU
  College Station, Texas 77840

International Association of Family
Sociology
  Department of Sociology
  Northern Illinois University
  DeKalb, Illinois 60115

National Council on Family Relations
  1219 University Avenue, SE
  Minneapolis, Minnesota 55414

Rural Sociological Society
  Department of Agricultural
  Economics
  University of Arkansas
  Fayetteville, Arkansas 72701

Society for American Archaeology
  5545 N.E. Skidmore
  Portland, Oregon 97218

Society for Applied Anthropology
  1703 New Hampshire Avenue, NW
  Washington, D.C. 20009

Society for Historical Archaeology
  c/o National Park Service
  143 South Third Street
  Philadelphia, Pennsylvania 19106

Society for Industrial Archaeology
  Room 5020, National Museum of
  American History
  Smithsonian Institution
  Washington, D.C. 20560

Society of Professional Archaeologists
  Department of Anthropology
  Washington University
  St. Louis, Missouri 63130

Index

Have You Seen These Other Publications from Peterson's Guides?

Peterson's Annual Guides/Careers
Engineering, Science, and Computer Jobs 1985
SIXTH EDITION
Editor: Christopher Billy

Gives up-to-date information on over 1,000 manufacturing, research, consulting, and government organizations currently hiring technical graduates. All the information in the book is brand-new and updated every year.

8½" x 11", 686 pages   Stock no. 2480
ISBN 0-87866-248-0   **$14.95** paperback

Peterson's Annual Guides/Careers
Business and Management Jobs 1985
Editor: Christopher Billy

This distinctive new career guide details hundreds of organizations that recruit employees in the nontechnical areas of business and management. In addition to giving specific information about each employer, the book tells applicants how to match their academic background to specific openings. December 1984.

8½" x 11", 400 pages (approx.)   Stock no. 2499
ISBN 0-87866-249-9   **$12.95** paperback

Liberal Arts Power!
How to Sell It on Your Résumé
Burton Jay Nadler

This is the first résumé book written exclusively for generalists, liberal arts students, recent graduates, and career changers. Using about 30 sample résumés, the author shows how job hunters can demonstrate their skills and match them to specific jobs. February 1985.

8½" x 11", 124 pages (approx.) Stock no. 2545
ISBN 0-87866-254-5   **$6.95** paperback

Jobs for English Majors and Other Smart People
John L. Munschauer

This book recognizes the realities of the job market for the generalist, the inexperienced, the career changer. The author offers down-to-earth advice about such common concerns as when to send and when not to send a résumé, how to identify alternative careers, and how to create a job when there is no advertised opening.

5½" x 8½", 180 pages   Stock no. 1441
ISBN 0-87866-144-1   **$6.95** paperback

Educators' Passport to International Jobs:
How to Find and Enjoy Employment Abroad
Rebecca Anthony and Gerald Roe

This book will help teachers and administrators explore realistically the benefits and challenges of finding an overseas job in the field of education. It tells educators how to find suitable employers and positions in the area where they want to work, create a résumé for the type of overseas job they want, interview for an overseas position, and more.

6" x 9", 196 pages   Stock no. 2715
ISBN 0-87866-271-5   **$9.95** paperback

The Independent Study Catalog:
NUCEA's Guide to Independent Study Through Correspondence Instruction 1983–1985
Editor: Joan H. Hunter

A new edition of the ultimate education "wishbook" for people who want to study on their own without the restrictions of regular class attendance. Students can choose from more than 12,000 correspondence courses offered by 72 colleges and universities. Credit and noncredit courses are available at the elementary, high school, undergraduate, and graduate levels.

8½" x 11", 120 pages   Stock no. 1808
ISBN 0-87866-180-8   **$5.95** paperback

Where to Start:
An Annotated Career-planning Bibliography
FOURTH EDITION, 1983–85
Madeline T. Rockcastle

This book is published by Cornell University's Career Center, which houses one of the best career libraries in the nation, and describes the career-planning publications used there. It covers books, periodicals, audiovisual resources, and other materials and is an invaluable tool for human resource managers, counselors, and librarians in both corporate and academic organizations.

8½" x 11", 206 pages   Stock no. 6260
ISBN 0-87866-260-X   **$11.95** paperback

How to Order

These publications are available from all good booksellers, or you may order direct from **Peterson's Guides, Dept. 4630, P.O. Box 2123, Princeton, New Jersey 08540.** Please note that prices are necessarily subject to change without notice.

- Enclose full payment for each book, plus postage and handling charges as follows:

Amount of Order	4th-Class Postage and Handling Charges
$1–$10	$1.25
$10.01–$20	$2.00
$20.01–$40	$3.00
$40.01 +	Add $1.00 shipping and handling for every additional $20 worth of books ordered.

Place your order TOLL-FREE by calling 800-225-0261 between 8:30 A.M. and 4:30 P.M. Eastern time, Monday through Friday. Telephone orders over $15 may be charged to your charge card; institutional and trade orders over $20 may be billed. From New Jersey, Alaska, Hawaii, and outside the United States, call 609-924-5338.

- For faster shipment via United Parcel Service (UPS), add $2.00 over and above the appropriate fourth-class book-rate charges listed.
- Bookstores and tax-exempt organizations should contact us for appropriate discounts.
- You may charge your order to VISA, MasterCard, or American Express. Minimum charge order: $15. Please include the name, account number, and validation and expiration dates for charge orders.
- New Jersey residents should add 6% sales tax to the cost of the books, excluding the postage and handling charge.
- Write for a free catalog describing all of our latest publications.

+

Copyright © 2019 by Jeff Fromm
All rights reserved.
Published in the United States by Vicara Books.
VICARA BOOKS | www.vicarabooks.com
All trademarks are the property of their respective companies.
Design and illustrations by Barkley Design & Experience
Cataloging-in-Publication Data is on file with the Library of Congress.
ISBN: 978-1-940858999
Proudly Printed in the USA

Special Sales
Vicara Books are available at a special discount for bulk purchases, for sales promotions and premiums, or for use in corporate training programs. Special editions, including personalized covers, a custom foreword, corporate imprints, and bonus content are also available.